T0147172

FINANCIAL FREEDOM

SECRETS OF DEBT-FREE LIVING

SIMON ARANONU

WESTBOW
PRESS®
A DIVISION OF THOMAS NELSON
& ZONDERVAN

WestBow Press books may be ordered through booksellers or by contacting:

WestBow Press
A Division of Thomas Nelson & Zondervan
1663 Liberty Drive
Bloomington, IN 47403
www.westbowpress.com
1 (866) 928-1240

ISBN: 978-1-9736-7555-6 (sc)
ISBN: 978-1-9736-7554-9 (e)

Library of Congress Control Number: 2019914930

Print information available on the last page.

WestBow Press rev. date: 01/07/2020

CONTENTS

PREFACE

Many people seem to be locked up in the prison of financial bondage. Some are serving short sentences; others are serving medium-term sentences; painfully, a great majority are serving life-term sentences.

Financial bondage could arise due to parental lapses. For example, some parents fail in their duty to properly educate, guide, or counsel their children. Parents sometimes erroneously give their children the impression that the society or government is responsible for the financial challenges they face. Children who embrace these thoughts could end up rebelling against society for no just cause. The energy they should apply positively to get out of financial bondage is then dissipated fighting against society.

On the other hand, some other people are in financial bondage due to debts left behind by their parents. Although, legally, a debtor is contractually obligated to pay his or her debts, there are various reasons why it is beneficial for children to take up the responsibility to discharge the debts of their parents. First, a family name is attached to an unpaid loan. And a bad credit search could make a bank or a lender reluctant to extend new loans if they believe it is in the family tradition not to repay loans. This is because character or integrity is the key philosophy that guides creditors in extending credit facilities. Additionally, if a child wants to utilize an asset purchased by a late or bankrupt parent, it becomes obligatory that they must continue to discharge the debts associated with that asset. For example, if a person lives in a house on which the late parents have unpaid mortgage obligations, it is imperative to keep paying that debt to enable ultimate ownership of the asset.

It is therefore possible that young people could find themselves saddled with a debt burden early in their career for different reasons. Some may need to refinance the old debt with a new one, especially if there is a possibility of a longer repayment tenor and a lower interest rate.

Compare a young person with the above background alongside another young person who has debt-free assets bequeathed to him or her, such as a house or quoted stocks.

In 1992 I attended a course in Long Island City, New York, where one of the facilitators shared with us how his father willed him a debt-free house. As soon as he started working, he sold the house to buy another house for himself. With this legacy, there is a strong likelihood that he will do the same for his children.

Another major source of financial bondage is self-inflicted. Many people make careless financial decisions that place them in bondage. Sometimes it's related to greed. For example, just before the economic meltdown and the ensuing real estate crisis of 2008, it was commonplace for finance people to take multiple mortgage loans for speculative reasons. When the bubble burst, they naturally entered into a long-term debt crisis. Some had even taken cross-border multicurrency risks by purchasing homes in currencies different from that in which they earned their regular incomes. This added another layer of financial risk to their debt obligations while also exposing them to regulatory risks in the various countries.

Financial bondage can be prevented. This book will guide you to identify and avoid possible factors that could lead to debt bondage. It also provides insight on practical action steps to exit an existing debt problem and offers strategic solutions on how to remain debt free on a sustainable basis. Finally, this book will provide you with guidelines on how to build and preserve personal wealth. The aim is to help you live a financially independent and debt-free life.

ACKNOWLEDGMENTS

I thank the Almighty God for inspiring this work and providing amazing answers to questions that appear to defy solutions. I appreciate my wonderful wife for letting me stay awake over several late nights as the thoughts and initial drafts of the book were being put together.

I deeply appreciate Suzette Anderson for her encouragement. Many thanks to my personal assistant, Mike Maduagwu, for his marvelous work in retyping the manuscript.

Finally, I owe a debt of gratitude to Modupe Olorunjo for initial editing and critiquing of this book.

CHAPTER 1

HIGHWAYS TO FINANCIAL BONDAGE

Financial bondage is a situation whereby debt becomes a lifestyle, and the debtor finds it challenging, if not impossible, to discharge debt obligations on a permanent basis. In this condition, even if a previous debt is paid, the debtor would soon contract a new debt to replace the discharged debt. The debtor is permanently dependent on debt for his or her sustenance.

I will detail twenty-one actions and factors that could create this trap. We must be circumspect to focus on avoiding them entirely.

1. IGNORANCE

The fastest way to become exposed to financial problems is through ignorance. Failure to understand financial matters leads to expensive errors. Finance is almost as important as blood because it is essential to enable one to provide for a family, obtain a quality education, own and furnish a home, and enjoy excellent medical care. Without finance, you cannot enjoy vacations to beautiful destinations or have a quality retirement.

If finance is so critical to life, why do many people have very little knowledge about finance, a factor that affects every aspect of life? There are rules and principles to investment and properly handling finance, and you should acquaint yourself with them.

It is therefore advisable to read books on finance. Nobody should take money and finance for granted. Money does not stroll into a bank account and remain there by wishful thinking. A person does not become rich or self-sufficient by accident.

People who make money accidentally often lose it because they are ignorant of the principles of finance. Stories abound of professional athletes, entertainers, and lottery winners who make quick bucks and still end up in debt. Some people inherit wealth but still end up in financial bondage for life. Such are referred to as having been born with "silver spoons." Yet there are folks who were born with no spoons at all but end up avoiding the debt trap.

One way to be successful is to learn from those who are successful and also from those who have failed so that we can avoid their mistakes. You can be forgiven when you make errors that no one has ever committed before. You cannot be forgiven for repeating the mistakes people have made and that are documented in books.

Please seek financial knowledge to liberate yourself from the shackles of financial captivity. Ignorance guarantees financial bondage while knowledge equips a person to exit the trap of financial bondage. Stop flipping away from television channels that broadcast business or financial news. It is strange that people pick up a newspaper on Monday morning and start with the sports page. Mondays through Fridays are business days! Why focus on entertainment and sports during the business week? Why not think business and finance?

Get to know what is happening on Wall Street because what happens on Wall Street ultimately affects Main Street. Study local and international trade, and understand macroeconomic issues. Read about official economic statistics published by the Fed. Attend training programs focused on finance for nonfinance people. Keep searching for financial knowledge. The fact that you are reading this book indicates that you are ready for financial freedom.

2. FINANCIAL INDISCIPLINE

Many people get trapped in debt because they lack discipline. If people could be disciplined in maintaining a relationship with their spouse, in keeping appointments and being punctual to work, in the use of personal devices, in obeying traffic rules, and in regular physical exercises, then why not apply the same discipline to financial matters?

It is surprising how people are quick to buy the latest version of their device. With due respect to the smart guys in research and development of mobile phone companies, the added features on these devices are not significant enough to justify purchasing a new version. Most people utilize fewer than 25 percent of the features of their personal devices, yet they pay for 100 percent. Nobody refunds the money spent on the 75 percent not utilized!

Consider your clothing, footwear, and accessories. Must you always buy the latest version? Designer products are great if you are wealthy and can afford them without credit, but you should not spend money on designer products when you are still growing your wealth. There are good-quality unbranded versions of the same products. And if you must have them, why not wait for the promotional sales period that happens after the rich have paid the exorbitant prices required to generate the bulk of the manufacturers' profits?

How about luxuries? How expensive is your wristwatch, car, home, or furniture? I once heard the story of a man who bought an expensive suit from a luxury shop in London. He expected his friends to compliment him when he wore it for the first time, but he was amazed that no one noticed. He had to announce to them the cost and the designer brand, yet nobody cared.

How about nonessentials? There is a marketing principle called impulse buying. This is when purchases are made for emotional rather than rational reasons. Marketers know how to position those products at online and physical stores to make you want to buy them. Advertisers know how to evoke your emotions with pictures and videos that will compel you to reach for your credit or debit card and place orders. Take a look through your home. You will be amazed to find several items that you have never used and never really needed.

A popular African novel is titled *The Beautiful Ones Are Not Yet Born*. Do you know what that means? Better products have not yet been made. Many things we were fascinated with a few years ago have suddenly become old-fashioned. What you call luxury today may become ordinary tomorrow. Wait a little. Better products are not yet on the shelves. Wait until you can afford them without incurring extra debt.

3. LACK OF SAVINGS CULTURE

Show me a wealthy person, and I will show you a person who knows how to save. Savings may not be popular today because credit cards are everywhere. Before credit cards came into vogue, most people relied on savings and occasional consumer loans from commercial banks.

In those days, folks who could not save and could not access banks' consumer loans were exposed and stood out as poor. Today such people cover their poor savings attitude by relying on credit cards. The issue here is that when you rely on credit cards, you may become permanently entrapped in debt. You may lose your financial freedom the moment you are hooked on credit cards.

Don't get me wrong. Credit cards are good when utilized to take care of temporary emergency needs as a stopgap facility. However, there is no rationale behind using credit cards for holiday trips to expensive resorts or purchasing expensive assets that add little or no value. The principle is never to incur a credit card expense that you cannot fully pay off with the next month's salary. When you use a credit card that takes many months to pay, you become entrapped in debt.

The use of credit cards that may take you several months to pay back is, however, wise only on one condition: if you have a deposit or savings equivalent to the credit. Paying back on the credit card while your savings remain intact has the added advantage of helping you build a credit history that will assist you in the future.

Savings never go out of fashion. It's the old way (and still relevant way) of building wealth. You cannot invest what you have not saved. It's savings first, and then investment follows. Your investments can make you wealthy, either through capital appreciation or returns—or a combination of both. Our parents taught us to keep 10 percent of our earnings in savings. We buy piggy banks for our young children today to inculcate in them the culture of savings. Can you imagine how wealthy you would be today if you have been setting aside 10 percent of your earnings after taxes?

You might think that you don't earn enough to save. Nobody really earns enough because the richer you are, the higher your expenditure profile. For a person who owns an SUV or even a private jet, maintenance and running costs will naturally be higher than a person who owns a saloon car. The fact is that if you cannot save money when you earn little, you may also find it difficult to save when you earn more.

Most people upscale their lifestyles to reflect their additional income. This is the reason some people in the middle class have to enroll in Social Security when they lose their jobs. The setback may sometimes lead to depression, hard drug usage, or even suicide. None of these provide a solution to the problems that could have been avoided if the person had a savings cushion. Therefore, learn to save now; today is not too late to start.

4. "MY MERCEDES IS BIGGER THAN YOURS"

We live in a world where contentment is gradually going out of fashion. But contentment in reality is a great personal gain because it gives you satisfaction and personal fulfillment, keeps you prudent, and restrains you from careless spending.

However, there is a lot of individual competition these days. There is a rat race that leads nowhere. Many people want to show they have a better car, a better home, and better jewelry than their peers. There is unwritten and unspoken but intense rivalry among young people. They put each other under pressure. One of the fallouts of this unhealthy competition is expansion of credit. Traditional bank loans and more modern lines of credit absorb the pressure. The ultimate impact is expansion of the number of those in debt.

Please stop comparing yourself with others. Life is not a hundred-meter dash that you have to complete in less than ten seconds. Life is a marathon. You are not in competition with anyone. There is no guarantee that those that started life with a bang will end up far above you. Even if they do end up above you, they cannot live your life. Live your life. It's yours. Don't attempt to live someone else's life. Be content, and escape the debt trap.

Don't allow community and peer pressure to push you into a debt trap. You'll never know the reality of what's happening in other people's homes. The person you are trying to catch up with may not have the kind of bills you pay or the scope of financial responsibility you have. He may, for instance, be single while you are already married with two young children, and therefore your priorities are different. His priority may be to own an expensive exotic car and be a happy tenant. Your priority may be to own your own home early in life and utilize public transportation for now. Don't emulate anyone blindly without checking their circumstances and comparing with yours.

In conclusion, my question to you is this: Who is your mentor? Your mentor is expected to guide and counsel you. His or her circumstance may not be exactly the same as yours but he may be able to see what you cannot see for now. Delayed gratification is always the sweetest. Enjoy life at your own time and space. Escape the debt trap.

5. POOR FAMILY PLANNING

Take a look at the poorest people in the world. They have one thing in common, and that is exponential population growth. Some grow at over 5 percent per year with the implication that the population doubles every twenty years. Take a look at the most advanced countries of the world. Most of them have a declining population and even have to import labor from poorer countries.

Let's go further in our analysis. In every country of the world take a look at family statistics between the rich and the poor. On the average the rich have one child per family. Take a look at the poor families. The average in some countries is as high as four children per family.

A man with four children would have to share his resources between them. Imagine if that same man has only one child. Instead of sharing his resources four ways, he could utilize them to give the one child a better standard of living.

People fall into a debt trap because they borrow to attend college or because many household items that could have been acquired with cash are purchased with debt finance. These sometimes have their roots in the sharing of scarce resources to an unplanned large family.

Some erroneously believe that having several children is a sign of strength, and therefore in some societies a man could father up to seven children. I am personally a victim of this. People from the high-income developed world are not less fertile than the poor. Far from it, it's all about planning. A nation can be rich while many of its family constituents may be very poor. The simple logic behind "income per capita," which is a measure of gross domestic product divided by its population, is that the higher the population the lower the income per head.

You may have been a victim of this. But do not continue on that path. Please plan your family. Do not have more children than you are able to give life's best to. Don't set your children on the pathway of debt even before they are ready to face the world.

6. DEBT DIVERSION

In my lending career as a banker, I have observed that many borrowers who are unable to repay their debts diverted them for an unintended purpose.

When a banker gives funds for the purchase of raw materials, it should not be used for plant and machinery. Whereas a banker expects you to repay a loan given for raw materials inventory in less than twelve months (sometimes as short as ninety days), the same banker may allow up to ten years for the payback of a loan for plant and machinery. It all depends on the cash-flow projection analysis. Accordingly, when a borrower uses a short-term credit line for what should be financed with a long-term credit line, the problem of tenor mismatch arises. Then the borrower runs into murky waters.

I know of a particular case where a borrower was advanced money for basic working capital to be paid back over a short term. The borrower constructed buildings and acquired machinery with about 80 percent of those funds. I do not need to tell you that after ten years the borrower is still in debt.

Another case is where the borrower was advanced funds to import finished products for sale. This fellow imported the finished products and sold them, but instead of repaying the loan to that bank, he diverted the funds to another bank for the importation of machinery. His business growth idea was laudable, but the execution was fraught with danger and deception. Meanwhile, he kept lying to the creditor bank that he was yet to sell the imported products. In the intervening period many policy changes took place that did not favor the borrower, and more than ten years later the loan is still outstanding.

If you don't want to be entrapped in debt, please do not divert the proceeds of debt from the original intention or purpose for which it was given. If you have other needs, please approach your banker. Bankers are in a position to give professional counsel and additional funds if you satisfy the bank's conditions.

7. INVESTING IN VOLATILE ASSETS

There is a finance maxim called "the risk return rule." It simply means that the higher the risk, the higher the return. There are investments that provide moderate returns. A good example is Treasury bills and bonds. The returns are moderate because the risk of losing your capital is near zero.

However, there are some other investment outlets such as the stock market that promise very high returns. Nonetheless, there is no guarantee that you cannot lose your capital. It's close to gambling, and there are no guarantees. Such investments are said to be highly volatile. They could swing to any direction. You could become a millionaire investing in them. You could also lose all you have in life.

Borrowed funds, therefore, should not be put into a volatile investment. When the stock market or currency trading market crashes, you are likely to get into the debt trap. The real estate market is another example. It's a volatile market. Every market that is subject to speculation is potentially volatile.

Don't get me wrong. I am not recommending that you should not take risks. If you don't take risks, you are not going to be rich. However, you should never borrow to invest in a speculative market.

8. SKILLS GAP AND DEBT

Over twenty-eight years ago a particular distributor and wholesaler of certain brands of car paints was a customer of a bank. He purchased his goods from those who imported the products from Europe.

One day he decided to begin importation of the products himself. In the paint industry, car paints are distinguished by a combination of certain alphabets and numbers. His very first importation landed him in bankruptcy because he made a wrong import order by misapplying the alphabets. It turned out that what he ordered was "oven dried" paints used by car manufacturers, instead of "air dried" paints. He tried to sell the products to the car manufacturers but failed. He became a lifetime debtor to the bank.

The skills required to be a retailer are different from the skills required to be a manufacturer, wholesaler, or an importer or exporter. In my banking experience, I have seen people make very expensive mistakes because they got involved in businesses for which they were inadequately prepared. Every business has a trade secret. It may all seem simple from the outside. For example, setting up a restaurant may not be as simple as it appears.

Take your time to undergo skills training and apprenticeship. Get the theoretical and practical trainings necessary for that business. Get exposed. Learn from the best in the industry. Don't be in a hurry to set up yours until you are fully grounded in that business. Get the necessary licenses. Undergo appropriate tutelage. It's not a waste of time to undergo training and acquire relevant skills. After getting relevant skills, ensure you carry out feasibility and viability studies. A business that works well in a particular district may fail in another location. Many variables, including differential demography, differ from location to location. Work with experts. Don't take a plunge without a parachute, as this can only lead to disaster. Don't step out before you are ready. If you step out before you are ready, you will close shop before you make money. Please avoid the debt trap.

9. FAMILY FINANCE VS. BUSINESS FINANCE

Many privately owned and managed businesses with great potentials have closed up prematurely because the owners did not separate business income from personal income. This partly explains the high mortality rate among microenterprises and small enterprises in many parts of the world.

You may be the sole owner of a business. However, the income from that business is not yours to spend. Many do not even care to ascertain whether the business is making a profit or not. As long as there is daily revenue, the owner keeps dipping his hands into the till to solve his personal financial problems. He spends on school fees, home needs, and even holiday expenses, without confirming if the business is generating enough income to support the expensive lifestyle. Sooner or later the capital of the business becomes eroded, and the debt journey begins.

If you are running a privately owned microenterprise or small enterprise, the thing to do is to set a reasonable salary for all workers including yourself. Live within that salary. Ensure you keep proper records of accounts. Audit your business yearly (or even semiannually) to determine whether you're making profits or not. That will guide you to determine how much you should reinvest in the business before determining how much you can spend on family needs. This is one of the secrets of successful corporations. Learn to separate your personal expenses from your business expenses. If you don't consistently reinvest the profits you make back into your business, the long-term sustainability of that business will be in doubt.

10. WHO ARE YOUR FRIENDS?

The circle where you are found could affect your lifestyle. There is a need for you to be true to yourself. If you are from a low-income family bracket, why should your best friends be from the upper class, especially if they compel you to borrow to measure up to their spending levels?

Even when you move within your class, please be careful around those who spend carelessly on credit. There are people who just love luxury that they cannot afford, and you need to be careful around them.

In my first year in high school my father drew me close and left me with a message: "Whatever you do in this school, never forget whose son you are." That was in 1974. It's been forty-five years, but that statement still reverberates within me. In my undergraduate years I was lured to join certain elite clubs. But my father's warning was a restraining factor. Stop operating within the social circle that your finances cannot support. This singular decision can help you escape from the debt trap.

11. NEW BUSINESS AND DEBT

It's suicidal to start a new business venture with borrowed money. There are usually two sources of finance: debt capital and equity capital. Equity capital is the business owner's funds. Debt capital is borrowed money. It's always advisable to start a business with equity/own funds. As the business grows and begins to make money, you can take on debt to support the equity, and this is referred to as leveraging.

Before you leverage your business, you must be sure the cash flow from the business can repay the debt and interest within the time agreed with the creditor. The easiest way to know this is to look at the historical cash flows of the business over the years. Then you can project into the future using available statistics.

That is why it is not advisable to borrow money to start a business. You do not have historical cash flows to determine reasonably whether the business can pay the debt. Additionally, you do not know if the business will succeed or fail. If the business fails with the owner's funds, the owner can weep alone. However, losing the bank's money could destroy your credit history. Please exercise caution in taking on debt for new businesses.

12. WILLINGNESS TO REPAY A DEBT

In over thirty-five years of banking and financial consultancy, I have learned one key secret about potential borrowers. There is a way to know those who have no intention or desire to repay. When I make out an offer letter to a potential borrower, and he takes time to read every line, I know he has an intention to repay. Potential good borrowers like that will send the offer letters to their attorneys to carefully review and advise them before they execute. Except for circumstances beyond their control, such people will always meet their obligations.

However, whenever a potential borrower receives an offer letter and does not read it, and all he asks is that I should show him where to sign, I get worried. In most of these kinds of borrowers, the willingness to repay may be lacking. Even when they are able, the lack of willingness would not let them discharge their obligations. Quite often it starts with a small debt. In no distant time, they acquire more debts.

There are people who keep switching from one credit card to another. They keep paying paltry amounts into the massive debts incurred with each credit card. By so doing they give a false impression to the card issuers. When all their debts are aggregated, it becomes obvious that they will never be in a position to pay off all the debts. Such people remain entangled in debt for a long time.

It takes extra self-control to manage someone else's money—otherwise called debt. If you lack self-control or the integrity, don't get involved in borrowing. As a banker, I've been lending billions all my life. I have been encouraging individuals and corporations to borrow to support their business. That's my job. But I find it difficult to sleep well at night when I borrow. Until I pay off any debt, I don't have peace of mind. Know yourself. Understand yourself. Self-control is key to discharging debt obligations. If you don't have self-control, do not borrow. If you have no willingness to repay, do not borrow.

13. PURPOSE OF DEBT

When you borrow money, what is the purpose of the debt? If you borrow money to go to college, it's a good investment. You will eventually come out with a degree and get a good job. Your future cash flow will eventually be good enough to repay the college loan. If you borrow to buy a vehicle that will be released to an über driver, over time, the cost of the vehicle will be repaid. The debt will be paid back. If you borrow to buy a home, it will save you the cost of the rent that you would have been paying if you did not own your home. The rent savings is an indirect cash flow.

If, however you borrow money to buy fashion accessories, electronic equipment to produce theater-type sound in your home, or to replace your furniture, it is not financially prudent. If your washing machines and clothes dryers can be fixed, it makes sense to fix them rather than buy a new set on credit. All the above expenses are called consumption expenses rather than investment expenses.

The test is to ask yourself what is the secondhand value of the item you want to purchase. If the item has little or no secondary market value, it does not make sense to purchase it with credit. For example, when you buy clothing or shoes, those items have zero secondary values. Nobody will buy them from you after you have used them. They are referred to as "wasting assets." They begin to lose value from the time you depart the shop where you bought them. Compare them with some investment assets, such as land and buildings, which often appreciate in value over time.

Don't borrow for wasting assets, assets that have an alternative, or assets that cannot confer additional cash flows either now or in the future. Rather, focus on acquiring investment assets that generate cash flows to repay the investment debt.

14. THE POWER OF POSITIVITY

Do you know that as a man thinks in his heart, so is he? If a person thinks positively, that person will act positively. A person who thinks negatively is likely act negatively. If you are in debt, and you believe you will come out of it, nothing will stop you from coming out of it. I mean absolutely nothing will stop you.

The secret is that when you think positively you will marshal a set of actions that will bring you out of debt. Additionally, positive thinking will energize you and provide you with the passion and drive required to run your financial life or business. The drive to run your business flows from positive thoughts. It leads you to go out believing you will win and that today will be better than yesterday. You have to believe that you will make the right connections and relationships. Never stay home feeling defeated. Don't give up, and don't succumb to self-pity. Forget the pains and failures of yesterday and remain confident that the odds will favor you.

If you apply this approach, new ideas will begin to flood your mind. You will suddenly attract the right people around you. An English proverb says that birds of the same feather flock together. When you are in debt, don't go around befriending fellow debtors who cannot repay their debts. Don't flock around complainants who always blame the system. Don't stay with those who have given up hope. Part of being positive is that you will confess positivity. Every word that comes out of you will be loaded with hope of a better future. You cannot get what you cannot see. You must see it in your inner mind first before you get it in the physical realm. That's how it works. Every skyscraper was once a vision in the mind of an architect before he drew the plans. Then the builders put it together. This principle drives everything in life, including becoming debt free. If you see yourself becoming debt free one day, it will be actualized.

On the other hand, if you think negatively and live negatively, you are likely to take actions that will place you in debt. The truth is that negative thinking robs you of great ideas while lack of great ideas creates a vacuum of positive actions. The ultimate result will then be poor financial outcomes, poverty, and financial gaps. Then you will have no option but to resort to debt to cover the gaps. Think positively, and act positively.

15. ADVERSE MACROECONOMIC FACTORS

An economic downturn hurts businesses. It hurts those in debt most because revenues will suddenly plummet through no fault of theirs while debt obligations remain unchanged.

Remember the global economic recession in 2008. World money markets, capital markets, and real estate markets collapsed, while credit dried up. Foreign currency markets went under, while layoffs abounded globally. Gross domestic products of most countries nosedived, and fiscal resources went south.

The impact of all these on personal debt was disastrous. Many people could not discharge their debts. Most homes were placed on sale by creditor banks. There were very few buyers. Property rates hit rock bottom. Those that had mortgage loans could not repay their debts, and many lost the equities in their mortgage loans. Those who had more than one home loan felt the impact more. More than ten years after, some people are still burdened with debts arising from the sudden market crash.

My advice is to reasonably mitigate your risks at all times. You must take risks if you want to grow and make wealth. However, you must always provide for a fallback position. When bankers lend money, they will always request "a second way out." It is expected that there must be at least two independent sources of repayment before loans are extended. This is to ensure that in the unlikely event of the primary source of repayment failing, there is a robust secondary source. If a banker cannot see these sources, he is not likely to extend the loan.

You can apply the principle to yourself. You should ask yourself whether you have an alternative or secondary source of repayment if one fails. If you cannot see it, don't borrow. Additionally, I advise you to mitigate your risks. Cover yourself. Don't take unprotected risks. For example, if you take cross-currency risks, ensure you hedge the risks. Don't stretch your luck.

Another way you can mitigate your risks in the case of unexpected recession is to diversify your investments. All those who invested heavily in the stock market lost heavily, and most got entangled into heavy debt. However, those that diversified into various assets were able to come back faster. You can keep your investment diversified into either real estate; marketable securities, including federal bonds and Treasury bills; stable foreign currencies; local currencies; or long-established reliable stocks. Develop a hybrid of investment portfolios. You will absorb macroeconomic shocks better if you do so.

16. FAILURE TO ADAPT TO CHANGE

Failure to adapt to change can place you in debt. We live in a highly dynamic ever-changing world. Cheaper and better ways of doing things are constantly being developed. Adapting to newer and better ways of doing things gives rise to efficiencies. Efficiencies imply improved and better results with lower inputs leading to improved margins and more profits.

On the other hand, ignoring change may lead to growing inefficiency, where cost of production or service delivery becomes disproportionately high relative to competition. The consequence is possible loss of market share and revenues while costs remain high. When revenue keeps declining and you cannot drive down costs, you will soon find yourself resorting to debt to bridge the gap.

Adapt to change but don't change for the sake of it. Do your math. Be sure of the incremental benefits of change and compare it with the incremental cost. Change is not always worth it. Furthermore, even when you need to implement change, consider various options available. For example, if you must buy new, more efficient machinery you may consider both the lease or buy options. Obtain an expert financial opinion to help you decide.

Nonetheless, never ignore changes taking place in your profession. It may be costly if you ignore such changes. That could place you at the debt door.

17. LOVE FOR LUXURY

Excessive love for luxury can lead to debt. Some cannot control hunger and desire for bespoke products. They want designer furniture. They want to use golden cutlery or use designer underwear. They are obsessed with the upper-class standard for everything they use.

Please don't get me wrong. Top-quality products by first-class designers are good. If you can afford them, please buy them. However, I have found that the rich are more prudent than the poor. No wonder the English proverb says "empty vessels make the greatest noise." It's the poor that want to show off and make noise. The rich, who are fully loaded with wealth, are calm and less noisy.

Don't get obsessed with luxury. If you do, and you don't have sufficient money to sustain that lifestyle, you will be compelled to rely on debt. If you don't contain the penchant for luxury, you may never exit the debt bondage.

This is because by the time you finish paying the first debt a new luxury product will be manufactured that you will again find attractive. Please stay away from the excessive love for luxury if you desire to live debt free.

18. FEEDING PAST GLORY

There are people who come from hitherto rich and wealthy parents and who grew up living like princes and princesses. Suddenly their parents experienced "professional accidents," and their income sources collapsed. However, they kept living that old life. Naturally, after some time, it becomes impossible to sustain that lifestyle without debt.

I heard of a man who was so rich that his children flew first class all over the world. At a point in time they even owned a private jet. They lived like royalty. They mingled with the high and mighty. However, when their father lost his wealth, they found it difficult to accept that reality. They began to borrow from friends who did not know their business had collapsed. Very soon they could not honor those obligations. Then they started disposing of their assets. When the assets were exhausted, they started borrowing from banks. Debts piled up simply because they could not accept the painful reality that the family business empire had collapsed.

If your income declines, don't try to sustain it artificially. You will only exacerbate your debt burdens if you attempt to sustain it by taking on more debt. I once lost my job, and my income plummeted badly. I called my children together and explained that we had to cut our expenses. I sold off my car. Every expenditure head at home was queried. When my income level turned around years afterward, the family lifestyle was readjusted accordingly.

Be realistic. Tell yourself the truth. Change your lifestyle when your income level changes. This way you can avoid debt.

19. DANGER OF LAZINESS

Laziness guarantees that you will get into debt, especially if you want to live like your peers. Laziness implies that a person will never produce at his or her best and that the person's output will be low.

The painful thing is that most people who are lazy love a good life. They want to live big. They sit down to watch movies in the daytime when they should be working. They are involved in entertainment and fun when their peers are working hard. As long as a person is lazy, poverty is guaranteed. If that fellow now decides to live a good life far above his income level, the only legitimate option would be to access debt.

20. POOR PRIORITIZATION

Inability to appropriately focus could place a person in debt. Some people are often bubbling with many ideas, and they start a project, but before the results begin to manifest, they begin another project. Their attention becomes divided. At the end both projects may fail if they are not patient enough to nurture the projects to maturity. Accordingly, this can lead to reduced cash to sustain normal operations, and the company or individual may end up resorting to debt.

Sometimes people may get distracted by events happening around them. For example, if their friends are making money in a particular line of business, they defocus and cross over to the new business, for which they are not prepared. Some people may just lack the required concentration or discipline to remain in a line of business, fight on, and finish to execution. If you lack focus, you are a likely candidate for debt.

21. INTEGRITY FACTOR

A person who lacks integrity will always owe and will forever remain in the dungeon of debt. A dishonest fellow will keep borrowing and keep lying to his creditors. Sooner or later, the hidden truth will be known by the creditors. Then he will attempt to find new creditors to deceive; the debt chain becomes elongated, and it becomes even more difficult if not impossible to discharge the debt obligations.

I have seen some serial debtors who keep borrowing from one creditor to another. Sometimes they borrow from one creditor to repay an old creditor. Sometimes they attempt to change their identity and location or business. But the long arm of the law eventually catches up with them. The only painful thing is that before then, they would have hurt many creditors. If you don't trust yourself, do not borrow money. If you are a lender, never lend money to anyone that lacks integrity. The person will never repay you.

CHAPTER 2

PROFESSIONAL FINANCIAL ADVISERS

Various professionals specialize in different facets of finance. You can consult these experts for support depending on your unique need. Please note that it may be necessary to first consult a general practitioner, who will later refer you to a specialist if the need arises.

Consider the case of your health as an example. Various professionals specialize in different aspects of health. For example, we have general practitioners; surgeons; internal medicine experts; ear, nose, and throat experts; fertility experts; dental experts; physiological; pediatrics, etc. In the same vein, you need to enlist the services of financial advisers to assist you in various aspects of managing your personal finance. They are trained. They may cost you good money, but at the end of it all, you will realize that it is cheaper to hire a finance professional than to manage a financial problem that could lead to debt bondage.

Please also note that the counsel you will get will depend on which finance professional you consult. Each professional will naturally advise you of opportunities in his or her area of specialization. Having a general knowledge of each professional's disposition will help you understand his or her inclinations and assist you in choosing the right professional counselor in finance. Below are some of the finance professionals available to you.

1. COMMERCIAL BANKERS

Most of us maintain savings or current (checking) accounts. Those accounts are commonly available in commercial banks. They are the bank offices littered all around us. The primary objective of the commercial bank is to attract as many low-cost deposits as possible and provide short-term credit facilities that are handsomely priced in order to generate decent margins that will absorb its overheads and create profits for shareholders. They will therefore offer you consumer loans such as mortgages, home purchase loans, renovation loans, motor vehicle financing, and credit cards, etc.

The cost of credit facilities is generally high all over the world. From their name (commercial) you can tell that they engage in merchandise and trade finance for commercial gain. If you visit this category of banks with a proposal for infrastructure financing and megaprojects (such as bridges, roads, refineries, or airports) you should know you are talking to the wrong people. Additionally, you will need such funds for very long periods that could be for up to twenty years in some cases and at a low cost of borrowing. If you mistakenly consult a commercial banker for such funds, you may get the wrong funds for a right project.

2. INVESTMENT BANKERS

Wholesale bankers handle large funds for various corporations and high net worth individuals. They understand megafinance. They move funds around the globe in various multicrafted financial instruments that maximize wealth for their investors. You don't find them littered around your streets. You are likely to find them in Wall Street and other "high" streets around the world where they maintain and manage megafunds of pensions and insurance companies. They have access to long-term capital and can make equity and debt management investments across the world. They understand currency risks and hedging. They are not designed for a small-time private borrower.

3. DEVELOPMENT FINANCE INSTITUTION MANAGERS

Development finance institutions (DFIs) are focused on development. Institutions like the World Bank (and their private sector arm—the International Finance Corporation), International Monetary Fund, European Investment Bank, Asian Development Bank, African Development Bank, US Export Import Bank (USEXIM), and such like, offer developmental finance to would-be borrowers. Some of them (like the World Bank) deal directly with governments, but their private sector arm deal with private corporations. They provide long-term relatively cheaper finance for development. Those that need consumer loans need not waste time going there. However, if you work in private sector corporations, you could approach such DFIs and access capital or even professional counsel. For example, a US corporation that wants to engage actively in export should approach the US EXIM bank not only for professional counseling but also for export guarantee lines that ensure sovereign risks of the importer countries are mitigated upfront.

4. MORTGAGE/REAL ESTATE BANKERS

These banks focus only on real estate. They are your best advisers if you want to engage in real estate ownership or business. They understand how to provide finance for real estate, as they have real estate licensed professionals who understand the market. You are not likely to get it wrong if you engage with the right professionals in this space before commencing negotiation on real estate acquisition or sale.

Commercial banks have real estate desks manned by experienced professionals. However, you should also engage real estate professionals who have hands-on and practical experience in the market. However, I advise that you exercise caution; sometimes they may be more focused on making a sale, with their primary motivation being their agency fees.

If you also want to sell a property, they can provide information. The same is applicable on renovations. When it comes to taking a second equity or third equity on real estate, talk to your real estate banker or the real estate desk of your commercial banks. When you are making an investment decision, be sure to expect that your real estate agent will recommend your purchase. Nonetheless the location is key. It determines the ultimate value and the resale price. Your personal wealth could be determined by the professional counsel you receive before you invest in real estate. Don't ever be in a hurry on investment decisions in real estate. The principle is the same rule you were taught in elementary school by your teacher concerning crossing the roads: "Look left, look right, look left again … then move across."

5. STOCKBROKERS

One way to build wealth is to purchase stocks. You can purchase equity stocks directly or through mutual funds (which are a blend of different instruments). You can preserve wealth through equities or even grow it through capital appreciation or returns on such investments. But many people have also become extremely poor by investing in equities.

You must always bear in mind the risk return rule; the higher the risk, the higher the returns. There are stocks that are very risky, but they also provide a window for high returns. In the same vein they provide the window for high capital losses.

However, you could also explore mutual funds. Some guarantee preservation of capital, while others may not guarantee preservation of your initial investment but could handsomely pay off in the short run.

What is your investment horizon? Are you buying to hold for a long time or are you buying to resell and make money and return to the market? The risk appetite of a young person in his/her twenties is obviously different from the risk appetite of a fifty-year-old who has two children in college.

The solution lies in obtaining wise professional counsel from your experienced stockbroker. Engage him. Pay him his fees. His fees are part of the investment you need to make to build personal wealth.

6. PENSION MANAGERS

Notwithstanding how hard-working you are, you will retire one day. Even if you don't want to retire, laws, regulations, or company policy will compel you to. Sometimes it's nature that may compel you to retire, as your physical body may no longer be able to cope with the stress of your job.

In 1992 I attended training at a school of banking in Long Island City, New York. As I intermingled with some of the fresh hires I got a rude shock. They told me that on the first week of their resumption at work (fresh from college), each of them was assigned "retirement advisers." It makes so much sense. If you are to plan your retirement, the planning should start on your first day at work. I mean, while you are still in your early twenties. Most people never think about retirement until a few years before retirement. They are too busy to think about it. That's why many people have taken nonpensionable jobs in their youthful years only to find out pretty late that they wasted those years.

Do you have an idea of how much you will earn as pension when you retire? Will it be enough to pay your bills, including your mortgage? How old will your child be when you turn sixty? If you are becoming a parent at the age of fifty, how old do you think you will be when that child is finishing elementary school? If your child is in junior high when you are retiring, how will that child get into college and acquire a degree? If you buy your first house at forty-five (and you have taken a thirty-year mortgage) are you aware that at sixty-five, you still have a ten-year mortgage to repay on that home loan? If you have retired at sixty-five, how do you repay the mortgage?

You need a pension manager to help you plan your retirement. It may cost some money to hire one. But believe me, if you don't want to retire in frustration, you need a pension/retirement professional. Get one now. You will be glad you did.

7. INSURANCE MANAGERS

The world is filled with risks. Nobody can accurately forecast what could happen tomorrow. Properties could be lost. Disability could come. Sicknesses could occur. Even life could be lost unexpectedly.

You need insurance experts to advise you on how to buy insurance. You need health insurance for you and your family, insurance for your vehicles in case of accidents, and you need to insure your home against fire, earthquake, flooding, tsunamis, etc. I know you may say your house is not prone to those natural calamities, but climate change is more real than you can imagine. Adverse natural disasters are being recorded in places no one expected. Therefore, buy good insurance from reputable insurance companies to preserve your wealth and avoid financial shocks.

Insurance companies offer all kinds of policies that could help you also build wealth. First, it's a good platform for compulsory savings. There are endowment policies that pay you lump sums as you attain certain ages. There are education insurance policies that can help you substantially defray the cost of college education for your children.

Insurance companies offer far more than you think. Let them help you buy critical insurance policies. Again, they may charge for their professional fees but the returns to your personal wealth will far outweigh the costs.

8. SOLICITORS

You need legal attorneys to be your personal advisers if you are to build wealth that will endure. The finance space is filled with traps that could very easily lead to mistakes and problems.

We all sign contracts regularly. We sign with our bankers, insurance companies, and landlords and tenants. We sign online contracts. Sometimes we read and sign believing that we understand the details. Always check the various forms and contracts you sign. Most have a clause requesting you to affirm that you have read and understand what you've signed; ensure you do.

What appears simple may mean various things in law. Please get a personal attorney. Retain one. If you are not satisfied with the one you have, fire him and get another experienced one. Please do not sign any contract without passing it through your solicitor. He will have the eagle eye to identify and sniff out hidden clauses that could hurt you financially and otherwise. Do not consider anything too insignificant when it comes to contracts. This covers every aspect of life, including job enrollment.

9. TAX CONSULTANTS

You need tax consultants if you want to build wealth. Ignorance is not an acceptable excuse in law. Tax consultants can help you understand tax laws and practice and can also guide you in completing tax returns. They will advise you on how to treat expenses and donations for tax purposes. There are various expenses not allowable by the tax authorities in computing your tax liability. Why do some people pay huge tax liabilities whereas some pay less? The difference is in professional counsel. Never evade tax. It's a criminal offense. But you can seek professional counsel who will help you comply with the law.

10. CHARTERED/CERTIFIED ACCOUNTANTS

Certified public accountants (USA) or chartered accountants (Europe) are good with financial figures. They are trained to provide accounting and audit services, among other things. If you need to properly audit your books, you need certified accountants. They will help you review your financial operations and audit them for the use of third parties. You can also retain one to keep your financial records in order to meet a minimum acceptable standard of accounting that will be acceptable by the auditors.

You can also engage them to provide consultancy services that can assist you to properly organize your business and make it more efficient while building a sufficient internal control mechanism that will eliminate losses and prevent fraud.

Hire professional accountants. You need accountants to succeed.

CHAPTER 3

UNDERSTANDING FINANCE

Finance is not complicated and can be understood by nonfinance people. Understanding the logic and language of finance will help you make sound financial decisions. Financial accounting was designed for business enterprises such as sole proprietorship, partnerships, joint ventures, and corporations. Unfortunately, finance knowledge seems to reside only with finance people. Meanwhile every one of us is involved with finance. Nonfinance people should therefore understand basic issues about finance to ensure they are self-accounting. Interestingly, there are issues in corporate finance that are applicable to personal finance.

Lessons we can learn from corporate finance can help us in personal finance. Here are some of them.

1. ASSETS

Assets are anything owned by a company and from which the company can derive benefits either now or in the future. In a typical corporation such assets can be classified as either current (short liquidating assets) or long term (expected to be in use beyond one year).

Current assets include cash, inventory, accounts receivables, and other near cash items such as Treasury bills and marketable securities.

Fixed or long-term assets include items such as land, building, plant and machinery, fixtures and fittings, etc. The bigger the assets of a corporation are, the bigger the corporation is. Additionally, it is the efficient use of the assets that guarantees substantial profits for corporations.

A company that has no assets cannot generate revenue or profits. This principle applies to personal finance too. Examples of personal assets could be physical assets such as cash, liquid assets such as marketable securities or even intellectual property rights. Cash can be invested to grow wealth. Marketable securities can be kept or sold to generate cash to invest in other assets. If people owe you, they are holding your assets. You need to collect your receivables to invest them. Anyone who delays in paying you is denying you of wealth creation. Don't be shy to collect your receivables now.

How about long-term assets? Take a look at your household items. You will not know their value until you organize a garage sale. All your furniture, including debt-free air conditioners, washing machines, dryers, television sets, etc. are assets. Your debt-free cars are your assets. You can sell them to generate cash to invest in assets that will produce wealth.

The only difference between the assets of a corporation and those of individuals is that corporations deploy their assets to produce profits whereas individuals sometimes invest in assets with little or no financial returns. Run your life like a corporation until you build enough wealth. Corporations do not set up foundations and engage heavily in corporate social responsibility when they have not even made money. Build wealth first before you begin to have fun.

Don't invest in wasting assets at the early stage of building wealth. Most household assets purchased for personal use, including motor vehicles and fashion items, are wasting assets.

Land and building are not wasting asset, but rather they are a good store of value. Examples of other assets that are a good store of value are precious metals or minerals such as gold or diamonds, short-term marketable securities issued by gilt-edged borrowers like the Federal Reserve Bank and other reputable governments, and fixed deposits in Federal Deposit Insurance (FDIC) insured banks that earn rates above inflation rates. Nonetheless always consult your financial adviser as mentioned in chapter 2 before you acquire assets, especially those that are substantial and are of a long-term nature.

Companies keep cash and near cash items in order to meet what corporations refer to as working capital needs. These are needs that come up from time to time for payment of supplies of essential inputs and payment of salaries, etc. In the same vein, you also need to keep reasonable cash and near cash items to pay your bills. If you invest all your revenue in long-term assets, you could become cash strapped and unable to meet short-term obligations such as your monthly utility bills, car lease, mortgage, insurance, etc. These must be paid when they fall due.

Please note that corporations also have contingency short-term overdraft lines (notes payables) to make up for occasional unexpected shortfalls in meeting their working capital needs. This will ensure that production or service delivery is not disrupted. In the same vein, you may need to set up contingency credit lines with your bank. This should be preferably covered with savings or fixed deposits as mentioned in chapter 1. This arrangement will help you avoid personal financial embarrassment when you cannot pay your bills.

Generally, it's great to acquire more nonwasting assets. Invest in longer-term assets, as they are a better store of value and could be sold to generate cash in severe exceptional circumstances.

2. LIABILITIES

Liabilities are obligations a corporation owes to third parties. It's the complete opposite of assets. In corporations they are classified into two categories: short term and long term. Short-term liabilities are those obligations falling due within twelve months. Accountants expect that you must pay them off within twelve months from the date they are contracted. They include trade account payables, accrued expenses, short-term borrowings such as overdrafts and notes payable, taxes payable, etc. The long-term liabilities are long-term obligations often due and payable beyond one year. They include long-term borrowings such as term loans, debentures, and any obligations that have more than one-year maturity.

We can apply the same principle to personal finance. Corporations try to extend payment of short-term obligations such as trade payables. They often negotiate with their suppliers to extend the payment date for as long as possible. The longer the tenor of trade payables the better it is for the corporations, as it provides a spontaneous financing source. The benefits are fantastic, as it becomes interest-free credit provided by the suppliers. The corporation is literally trading with the supplier's interest-free credit, which automatically becomes a funding source. In the same way, the longer you can defer your obligations, the cheaper it is for you. That's why your bills arrive monthly. If you can get contracts for utilities that will offer you longer-term payments, you can save money by investing the excess cash.

Furthermore, corporations need long-term borrowing to acquire long-term assets. In the same manner, you should not use short-term borrowings to finance long-lasting assets such as real estate. If you do so, you will run into a tenor mismatch problem due to the fact that the cash flows from the assets cannot be sufficient to repay the loan. That's why mortgage companies and banks could provide loans with a tenor of up to thirty years to finance real estate.

Generally, corporations would like to avoid incurring liabilities, but that cannot be eliminated in business. However, the smaller the liabilities, the better the financial health of the corporation. I advise you to also incur fewer liabilities. Liabilities lay claim on the assets. It's the assets you own that you often liquidate to pay liabilities. Therefore, the fewer your liabilities, the smaller the claim is over your personal assets. Except when you are borrowing to acquire long-term high-value income-generating assets, minimize your debts. It's unacceptable if you incur debts for personal fun.

3. NET WORTH

In accounting for corporations there is a financial record called the balance sheet, which is the statement of financial position.

The balance sheet of a company has three major items: assets, liabilities, and net worth.

If you deduct the liabilities (what the company owes) from the corporation assets (what the corporation owns) the difference is called the net worth. Mathematically the net worth is derived as follows:

$$Assets - Liabilities = Net\ Worth$$

In other words, when a company deducts what it owes (liabilities) to third parties from what it owns (assets) then the balance of the assets is what belongs to the owners (shareholders). That's the net worth of the company.

The net worth determines the value of a company, especially in times of liquidation or mergers and acquisition. It can also contribute in determining the stock market value of the company alongside other factors. Generally, the higher the net worth of a corporation the higher the value, all other things being equal.

In the same vein, individuals have a net worth. This could be represented in a simple statement indicating all your assets alongside your liabilities and ending with the net worth.

The higher your net worth the richer you are. In essence it's not just what you own that matters but also what you owe. If you increase what you own without increasing what you owe at the same rate, you will be building wealth and escaping financial bondage. Let your increase in liabilities be at a far lower rate than the rate at which you increase your assets. If you achieve that, you will increase your net worth.

4. REVENUE

Another word for revenue is sales, and this is central to profit. For corporate accounts, revenue is calculated by multiplying units of products sold by the selling price of each product (after adjusting for discounts and returns). This therefore implies that you can push up revenue or sales by either increasing the quantity sold or increasing the selling price per unit or increasing both indices.

Revenue determines the market share and profitability of a corporation. The revenue also absorbs the cost of goods or services sold, leaving the gross margin.

The gross margin must cover the expenses incurred in running the corporation. It's after these costs are deducted that you can determine the profit or loss.

Generally speaking, the higher the revenue the higher the gross margin, especially if the cost of goods sold is increasing at a lower rate than the rate of increase of revenue. This produces a reasonable gross margin that could absorb the selling, general, and administration (SGA) expenses. That's how companies post decent profits and pay handsome dividends, and invariably the market value of their shares is enhanced.

Let's apply this to personal finance. How big is your revenue? Your revenue is the sum total of the income available to you including your salary. Are you maximizing your wages? Have you benchmarked fellow professionals? Do you earn the salary that your contemporaries earn? If you are working for yourself, do you charge the kind of fees your fellow professionals charge? If you are selling products or services, how many products do you sell compared to your peers? Do you have multiple sources of income or investments that complement your regular salary?

Companies push up their revenue to remain profitable. You must push up your personal revenue to remain wealthy. When you achieve this, your revenues will be robust enough to absorb your family expenses and leave you with a decent margin for savings. Then you can invest the savings, leading to multiple incomes. This cycle continues to repeat itself, making you even wealthier as long as you keep close control on your personal expenses.

5. EXPENSES (COST OF DOING BUSINESS)

Corporations have two major cost items—direct costs and indirect costs. Direct costs are the immediate costs directly connected to the production of goods and services. For example, in order to manufacture a tangible product a corporation will need raw materials, labor, electricity, and consumables. Some machinery will be expended in the factory. Those are direct costs. The lower these costs, the higher the gross margin.

The indirect costs are costs incidental to the business. They include wear and tear of machinery (called depreciation in finance), advertising expenses, vehicle running expenses, telephone expenses, and administration expenses. They are also referred to as selling, general, and administration (SGA) expenses. If you can reduce these costs to the barest minimum, you are on the way to posting a good profit as a corporation.

Individuals also have direct and indirect costs.

If you are running a restaurant, the wages to the chefs and stewards, the cost of the food, and the cost of gas are direct costs. If you must achieve high personal gross margins, you must keep these costs at the barest minimum without compromising the quality.

The cost of providing gas for distribution vehicles; cost of advertising; cost of electricity, telephones, and internet services; and salaries of security personnel are all indirect costs. Again, you must bring these costs to the lowest level for the restaurant to be profitable.

The secret of wealth creation and escaping the debt trap is to drive up your revenues to the highest level possible and bring down your costs to the lowest level possible. If you are an employee, and you have already maximized your earnings by way of wages, you must do something radical about cutting down your direct and indirect costs in order to have profits. Part of your direct costs as an employee is the cost of transportation to and from the office. Have you reviewed all the options? Must you drive to the office daily? Do you have cheaper alternatives such as public transport—rail or bus? Can you consider shared rides? You may think it's nothing to fuel your car and drive to and from work. Do the math. Consider car fueling, maintenance, and parking fees. Add it up for one month. Compare it with public transportation costs. It may amaze you what you could save.

If you must drive (because there is no reliable public transport) have you reviewed the cost of fueling the car? Must you drive that four-liter four-wheel-drive that guzzles gas? Why not consider a smaller car?

Other direct costs for an employee include clothing and feeding costs. Where do you buy your lunch? Compare that with bringing lunch from home, which may not only be healthier but also far cheaper. Where do you buy your office wears? Can you search for and purchase anything online? Shop around. Look for the most cost-effective clothing. Nobody becomes rich by throwing money away.

A wealthy friend once told me that "money knows those that accommodate it comfortably. Therefore, if you spend money carelessly, money will notify its other colleagues and associates that they are not safe in your home. However, if you make money comfortable in your domain by keeping it safe in your bank accounts, that same money will notify other monies that they are safe under your roof. That way they will arrive easily and join their colleagues, and you will be rich." It sounds funny, but it works. Money literally has sense. It hangs around prudent people.

Consider some other personal indirect expenses such as cable television, heating, cooling, and house maintenance costs. Can you learn a few skills such as plumbing and carpentry so that you don't pay a lot of money on technicians to fix things in your home? Can you paint your home? Much more, can you control your mobile phone and electricity bills? Can you get a lawn mower and maintain your lawns? How many unnecessary trips do you make? How often do you eat out as against home cooking? One is definitely cheaper than the other. Watch your personal expenses. If you control your personal direct and indirect expenses, as corporations do, you are on your way to financial freedom.

Finally, when corporations bring down their cost of doing business and drive up their revenues they eventually make good profits. This is reflected in a profit and loss account. It's an account that reflects revenues on one side and reflects costs/expenses on another side. The net effect is either a profit or a loss. If revenues exceed costs the net effect is a profit. If costs/expenses exceed revenues the net effect is a loss.

If a company continues to make profits it will boost earnings and declare more dividends, and stock values continue to appreciate. Inversely, if a corporation continues to incur losses the stock value declines. If the losses eventually exceed the net worth (owner's funds) the company will be said to be in insolvency and stands the risk of liquidation.

In the same manner if a person continues to spend far less than he or she earns, that will lead to an accumulation of wealth. If, however a person consistently spends more than earnings, he or she can only continue to maintain that lifestyle by borrowing. That may be by way of a credit card. That is one way to enter into financial bondage.

6. FUNDS FLOW STATEMENT

Sometimes corporations prepare what is called a fund flow statement. It is often in the form of charts or histograms that pictorially indicate the various sources and uses of funds. It indicates where the revenue/incomes were generated from and how they were utilized for various purposes in the corporation. The logic behind this is to know how to achieve prioritization. It indicates the 80/20 Pareto principle. It will pictorially show you where most of your income came from and guide you to place more emphasis on high-income areas. The expenditure side will also indicate where most of the funds were spent.

I advise you to go through this process as an individual. You need to know where most of your income is generated from. That will help you make critical decisions. For example, I have a friend who was working for a telecommunication company on a nine to five job. She, however, also provided catering services on weekends. One day, she realized she was making more money on the part-time weekend job than on the regular Monday to Friday job so she quit. Today, she has established successful restaurants making several times more than she earned from her salary.

In the same vein, review your expenses profile. Focus more attention on your biggest expenditure lines and work to cut them down. This way you end up having a decent profit in your individual profit and loss account. Then you can afford to pay yourself dividends.

CHAPTER 4

BUILDING ENDURING PERSONAL WEALTH

The wealthy don't rely on credit to meet their individual needs. They can draw on their existing wealth to meet their financial obligations. They don't fret when the monthly bills are delivered at the mailbox. They have enough cash or near cash reserves to clear the bills.

It is therefore important that you build wealth. It is necessary that you have a buffer of financial resources in order to live debt free.

However, building wealth will cost you some critical requirements. What we have done is to draw from the experiences of corporations in the ways and manners they built wealth. When faithfully applied in personal finance, it is likely to help you build wealth.

I will therefore share with you the ten Cs of building personal wealth.

1. CAPITAL

Capital is indispensable to building personal wealth. Capital is like a seed that is the beginning of wealth accumulation and deliverance from the debt trap. There are two forms of capital: owners' funds (equity) and debt (borrowed) funds. You cannot start any business with debt capital. It's never done. If you do so, the interest on borrowed money could suffocate the business. Shareholders can wait for years to collect their first dividends, but debt providers can't. Additionally, if you have to repay the principal portion of the borrowed money so soon, it could adversely affect the business. What if the business fails? If you lose your personal capital you can start again. If you lose the debt capital you could be entangled in a debt crisis.

Learn from corporations. No corporation is incorporated with borrowed money. The owners start the business with shareholders' funds, also known as equity. It's the initial net worth of the corporation. Over time as the corporation prospers, it could increase its trading capital by borrowing. This is called leveraging. By this time the corporation could forecast its cash flow and determine its capacity to absorb and pay back the debt over a certain period. Obviously as the corporation pays back, it builds a credit history that would encourage creditors to lend the corporation more money.

Personal finance is similar. Whatever business you want to engage in, please start with your own capital. And here is how to build personal capital. First, learn to save. Saving is not fun. Saving is not convenient. But one sure way to raise capital is through savings. You must start today no matter how small. And you must be consistent. Give it time. You will return back with a smile.

The second way to build capital is to handle unexpected inflows with caution. If you have a raise in pay or a performance bonus, do not raise your lifestyle. Lock up or invest those extra funds. The natural inclination is to go on a shopping spree. Resist that temptation. Set aside every bonus as future capital.

The third way to raise personal capital is to dispose of assets that are not yielding income. Carry out a personal audit of your assets. You may be amazed that you have some assets lying idle in your home that could be sold for cash.

Capital is critical to business wealth. Build it consistently in a disciplined manner. You will never regret it.

2. CAPACITY

Capacity means having the competencies and skill to run a business. You cannot handle carpentry work if you never learned it. You cannot handle plumbing works if you never trained for it. Whatever you need to do, acquire skills for it. Attend relevant schools. Make an effort to understand the secrets of that profession. Every profession has a secret. It may look very easy on the outside, but it may have many secrets when you get involved.

A friend of mine left banking to set up a chicken farm. He was doing pretty well. Within a short time, he had tens of thousands of chickens. One day he lamented to me in tears and could not be consoled. Why? A terrible bird flu attacked one of the birds, and in a few hours he lost all the birds. To make matters worse, he had no insurance over the farm. He paid a big price for the inability to acquire capacity.

Learn from corporations. Corporations spend a lot of money training their staff to acquire capacity. Capacity building is a standard culture in organizations. When I joined a subsidiary of Chase Manhattan Bank in 1987, I was trained for one year before I could join the lending team. I attended work daily, but the work was in the training school. Ever since then I have attended over two dozen training sessions at various business schools all over the world. Corporations also employ highly skilled manpower, even if it requires them paying a premium salary.

Learn from corporations. Acquire skills. Attend capacity enhancement sessions. Keep retraining. In our ever-changing world, new and more efficient ways of doing business keep evolving. You need to catch up with the changing dynamics of the environment. I am glad you got a copy of this book because by reading it you are building your capacity. You need capacity to handle money and to start a business or a job. You cannot handle any job beyond the capacity you already have.

3. CHARACTER

Character is who you are when no one else is looking over your shoulder. Character is your integrity and will determine if people can trust you.

Any corporation that is set up by dishonest people will never be sustainable. Any corporation that does not keep its word will soon be out of business. That's why corporations fire dishonest people as quickly as possible so that they do not contaminate the good ones.

There is nothing hidden that will not be revealed. It's only a matter of time. If you are fraudulent, it will soon be exposed. If you never comply with the law, very soon the long arm of the law will catch up with you. If you refuse to pay correct taxes it may not be long before you are caught. If you know you will ultimately be caught, why do it?

You may not know this, but bankers check the integrity of not only the directors of corporations and key management staff but also the key shareholders before they extend credit facilities to them. In the same manner, you need to build character. If you have character, people will trust you, and they could make available to you resources that could assist you in building wealth.

4. COMMITMENT

If you want to build wealth, you must be committed to building wealth. You must be committed to whatever job you are doing. There should be no half measures. You must give it your best. Another word for it is diligence. Any person that is diligent in his/her work will be found among kings and royalty.

Anyone who is lazy can never build wealth. Anyone that is successful in the daytime has worked hard in the nighttime. You must sacrifice pleasure for hard work in order to build wealth.

Consider corporations. You have a resumption time and closing time in your contract of employment. You must clock in and out electronically. You are given an identity card that you use to access various offices. Many employees do not know that any time they utilize their cards to access various doors they are basically being monitored. At the end of the month, management gets a detailed report showing who went where. They can tell how long you spent in your office without talking to you. That's why management may not permit you to use your personal cell phone in the workplace. What is the management trying to achieve? They want the employees to do the work for which they were employed and are being paid. They want diligent or committed people in the workplace. That's how they can produce results.

5. CURTAILMENT

Curtail wastage. Successful people do not waste anything. Over twenty years ago I accompanied a friend to visit a multimillionaire who lived in a massive expanse of property in New Jersey. We passed through three levels of security at different gates. By the time we were ushered into his home, he was busy in another room. Finally, he came in with apologies. Then he did something that shocked me. He said he was hungry. He opened his small refrigerator and brought out some leftover sardine fish and some slices of bread. He reluctantly offered us some, and we politely declined. I noticed that the leftover fish was carefully wrapped in a foil. After the meal, he again wrapped the leftover fish and carefully tucked it back into the refrigerator. That day I said to myself, "I see why rich men are rich."

It's unfortunate that a lot of people waste food, clothing, and also waste money on electronic devices. Some rich men fly economy on short-distance routes. The poor fly business class and have no savings. The rich buy medium-sized cars and remain rich. The poor buy luxury cars and waste money feeding luxuries. Many rich people cook at home or eat in reasonably priced restaurants. The poor waste their money in expensive restaurants. The rich and wise locate holiday resorts within the country and enjoy their vacations at low price. The poor want to travel overseas on expensive holiday trips using their credit cards.

Curtail your expenses. No one becomes rich by wasting money. Curtail your appetite for luxury. Let your lifestyle be modest and humble. A loud and noisy lifestyle will require a lot of money to be "oiled." You can do without it. Be wise. Be prudent. Curtail expenses.

6. COMMUNICATION

Be a communicator. Link up with friends and associates. Build a network of people and constantly relate to them. Don't stay alone. Don't live in your own world. Reach out to people in the community. Reach out to old classmates. Attend reunions. Attend family outings. Attend social gathering. Be visible. Be reachable.

Your real net worth is in the contacts on your cell phone. Your real net worth is in your mailing list. Your contact list is a reflection of your real worth. Those are people who can support you in more ways than one. They provide you information. If you are to set up a business, they are the first you can call on. They are your real champions who can recommend you to others. They are the ones who can speak about you. I am a beneficiary of networking. Most jobs I have done have been secured through referrals of associates and friends.

Corporations spend money advertising the organization and its various products. They engage in corporate social responsibilities. They strive to be visible. They maintain credible associates in every field. If corporations do it, you too should do the same.

7. CONFRONTATION

Confront challenges. Never run from challenges. I have a multimillionaire friend who is involved in the upstream sector of the oil and gas industry. I asked him to share some of his secrets of success with me. To my surprise, he told me that while others panic and run away from business challenges, he relishes in confronting them. He told me he has learned from experience that behind any major business challenge there is big money to be made. He therefore deploys all his resources to ensure that he confronts and conquers all the challenges.

Making money is not an ice cream party. Creating wealth is a battle. If creating wealth was very easy, everyone would be wealthy. But there will always be the poor in the land, because there will always be guys who love the easy path. There will always be guys who want to collect handouts or live on the benevolence of others. An African proverb says a man refuses to go to the farm because he is afraid a lion could be on the bush path. Meanwhile he stays home, afraid of the lion, and starves to death. He could have gone out to the farm and put structures in place to avoid the lion even if there was one.

Don't run away from your lions. Confront them. Corporations face obstacles too. They find ways around them without breaking the law. Corporations face stiff competition from rivals. They never back off. They engage in aggressive marketing and advertising to push their products through. They engage in research and development to be ahead of rivals. They face battles with suppliers and bankers and various stakeholders. They never give up. You too must never give up. Fight your way to financial success.

8. CAPTURE

Your wealth is determined by how far your products can be sold. Look at multinational corporations. They set up manufacturing plants all over the world for various strategic reasons and potential benefits. They want to capture market share. Consider the internet giants who own Amazon, Microsoft, Facebook, Google, and Twitter and consider service providers like über. They attempt to serve the world. Consider CNN; they broadcast to the whole world.

It's a simple strategy. The more consumers you capture, the richer you are. It's not complicated. If corporations use this principle it can work for you. Enlarge your coasts. Expand your job. Expand your business. Get more clients. Create more products. Give your consumers multiple options. Expand your business. Enlarge the frontiers. That's the way to make more money.

9. COUNSEL

In the multitude of counsel there is wisdom. You cannot be better than those that provide you counsel or advice. Consider large corporations. They are careful to select their boards of directors with unique qualities. They consider their intellect, professional standing, and experiences. They ensure the board meets regularly to provide counsel to management. In the same vein, they also carefully select an Executive Management Committee to guide the entire rank of the company staff.

If corporations need counselors, then you cannot build personal wealth without counselors. The beginning point is to get a mentor. We do need mentors. You need someone who will hold your hand. You need someone who may have passed the route before or something close to what you want to do. That person may caution you if you want to make mistakes and also has answers to questions you want to ask.

In the eastern part of Nigeria, there is a wealth creation and poverty eradication culture that many international agencies have commended in recent times. It works like this: A businessman, trader, or professional person hires young people as artisans who work with him/her as an apprentice learning the trade of business. This mentor/mentee arrangement lasts for between five to seven years. Within this period normal salaries are not paid. The mentor basically "saves" the salary for the mentee. The mentor, however, provides feeding and accommodation, clothing and health care free of charge for the mentee throughout the period of mentorship. After the preagreed period of apprenticeship, the mentor is obligated to release capital equivalent to or more than the uncollected wages to enable the mentee to set up a similar business. He will remain close to the mentee until he himself is successful enough to mentor others. This way capital and skills are passed down, and poverty is eliminated while providing jobs.

Get a mentor. Get regular wise counsel.

10. COMMERCIAL ORIENTATION

Most companies will conduct feasibility and viability studies before they embark on a project. These studies provide a forecast to indicate if the project would be profitable and viable.

Corporations prepare budgets. They strictly monitor their budgets. They want to make money. Any product line that does not produce decent margins is shut down. Loss-making regions are closed down.

There are no sentiments or emotion in building wealth. You should not invest where you are sure to lose money. In building private wealth, be sure you are commercially profitable. Don't take a job that will not cover your living expenses. It does not make sense except you have some other nonmonetary benefits known to you. Your job should be "profitable" and should not leave you worse off. Always consider the commercial benefits before you sign a contract. If this job or business does not leave you better off, why should you engage it? Be conscious of the fact that at the end of the day, everything you are doing must come down to the hard facts of figures.

CHAPTER 5

PRESERVING PERSONAL WEALTH

It is challenging to build wealth. Nonetheless it is more challenging to preserve wealth. There are many persons who were once wealthy or successful. It is very easy for wealth to literally develop wings and fly away.

Accordingly, wealth must be nurtured and cared for. Personal wealth must not be handled, spent, or invested carelessly.

Prudence is the key guiding principle in preserving wealth. Self-control is critical in preserving wealth. Personal wealth can be preserved for a lifetime if you follow certain fundamental principles. Here are some tips in preserving personal wealth.

1. PROTECT THE PRIMARY CASH FLOWS

A typical corporation will do everything possible to ensure that its product lines are not hindered in any way. Every corporation has various sources of cash and revenues. There will always be dominant products that generate the substantial cash flows. That is the cash cow of the company. If anything goes wrong with the dominant revenue source, the existence of the corporation may be called into question.

Let's take it to personal finance. If you are working as an employee, nothing precludes you from having other investments. That's the principle behind multiple streams of incomes. You can have a nine to five job and still purchase stocks in the capital market. You can still buy Treasury bonds. You can even release your car to über for purposes of making additional income while you utilize public transportation.

But your primary cash flow source remains your job. You know that over 80 percent of your income is from your job. You must therefore do everything within your power to protect your job. Nothing must conflict with your job. You must give it your best, and you must not be found wanting in your place of work. You must be aboveboard. You must be excellent in the discharge of your duties.

This way you will protect your dominant cash flows and preserve your wealth.

2. BUY INSURANCE

Corporations buy all kinds of insurance to preserve the corporation. They have motor vehicle insurance, fire insurance, and transit insurance to cover goods in transit. Some companies buy professional risk insurance against potential litigations. Some take out fidelity insurance on their staff. Smaller corporations take out key man risk insurance. Why do corporations buy all these types of insurance? For wealth preservation!

If corporations buy insurance, you too should buy some to achieve the same purpose. Insure your homes and cars. Insure your health. You can never over insure yourself and your assets. It's always cheaper to buy insurance than to attempt remedial actions after disaster. Please buy insurance.

3. COLLECT YOUR DEBTS

If you don't want to be in debt, you must collect your debts. I know of a billionaire who always pays his debts. He will do anything possible to honor his debt obligations and will never default. However, if anyone owes him, he will also collect those debts using any strategy at his disposal. That's why I respect him. No wonder he is a billionaire today.

It's the simple logic that I recommend for you. If your debtors do not pay you, very soon you will be in debt yourself. Don't let your debtors feel they can take your money and walk away. Even if the amount is very small, use every legal effort to collect your money. If one debtor refuses to repay you, and you do nothing about it, very soon word will go around that you are a weakling, and other debtors will also default. You can even spend a bigger sum of money to pursue the recovery of a smaller sum just to send a message that you are serious. Do not get sentimental or emotional when it comes to recovering your monies.

Corporations have debt recovery agents. Banks have loan recovery departments. Banks dispose of mortgaged assets in order to recover their debts. Corporations file litigations against delinquent debtors to recover their debts. Don't be lenient on debtors who want to ruin you. If your debtor has a genuine problem and has discussed plans to pay later, that is a different matter. However, whoever has the capacity to pay but is unwilling to pay must be made to pay within the ambit of the law.

4. STAFFING MATTERS

Be careful to assess the integrity of your staff because one easy way to lose wealth is through pilferage. Stories abound of rich people whose chauffeurs plunder their resources. How about housemaids who steal jewelry from their employers? Some stewards forge signatures of their bosses to steal funds. Much more dangerous are personal assistants and information technology assistants who could steal data and break into your accounts.

Corporations are careful who they hire. Some would hire only through trusted referrals while others insist on strong referees with character attestation. Despite these measures, corporations still set up internal audit and inspection departments to monitor potential fraudulent activities. They constantly look over the shoulders of their staff. They ensure segregation of duties and regular audits to avoid internal control risks. They keep reinventing the process flows to avoid collusion and other weaknesses of internal control.

If corporations do all these, you must do the same. Trust your personal staff but watch over them all. One more piece of advice is: do not hire anyone you cannot fire. Watch your personal staff. You must preserve your wealth.

5. COMPARATIVE THINKING

There is something I call comparative thinking. For every item in life there is always a cheaper alternative. This is one of the reasons why corporations go through a tender or bid process every time they want to purchase key items. The process is that they advertise for suppliers, who then submit sealed bids. The company sets up a committee to review the technical competences of each bidder, and the few that pass through this stage will qualify for commercial evaluation. This way, the best and cheapest supplier is selected. After this stage, the company still negotiates for more discounts and ensures that it never overpays for any procurement. The company is preserving wealth.

Do you shop around before you make purchases? Do you get value for your money? Courtesy of the internet we can compare prices and quality across the globe. Stop overpaying for your personal procurement. Every overpayment is a depletion of your wealth.

Related to this is the idea of alternative options. Everything you want to buy also has an alternative or substitute. A two-bedroom house will definitely be cheaper than a five-bedroom house. If you have one spouse and one child, why should you buy a five-bedroom house? If you have one spouse and one child, why should you buy a seven-seater minivan? It just does not add up. Please watch how you procure items. Save money, and preserve your wealth.

6. HEALTH AND FITNESS

Executives of large corporations enjoy amazing health benefits. They are encouraged to do regular health checkups. Many are registered with health clubs at the expense of the company. Many corporations have gyms and fitness centers in the building.

What are the companies trying to achieve? They want a healthy and fit workforce. Prevention is better than cure. When a staffer calls in sick, the man hours lost can lead to substantial losses in dollar terms. On the other hand, when executives and staff are in good health, their productivity will be obviously higher.

Learn from corporate organizations. Live healthy. Stay fit. Exercise regularly. Have a regular medical check done. If you are running your own business you can't afford to be sick for long. If you are out of the office unplanned or unprepared, many things can go wrong. I have a close relation who was running his own business with two attendants but then fell sick. While he was in the hospital, the attendants mismanaged the business. He had little or nothing left by the time he resumed. Watch your health. You can manage your business and personal finances better when you are in good health.

I've also seen cases where staff are fired because they persistently fall sick. The employer may not fire immediately but may wait for an opportune time. It may be during the appraisal, staff evaluation period, or during a general retrenchment exercise. A sickly person could easily be a prey. Remain fit. Be healthy and productive.

7. "LOCK AWAY" YOUR SAVINGS

In the olden days our ancestors saved money by ensuring that they opened their savings accounts in bank branches located very far away from their residences and places of work. That way it wasn't convenient to visit those bank branches to withdraw their savings. Some would hide their savings passbooks so that they would not be tempted to withdraw the funds. Our ancestors were good savers. Unfortunately, our generation of people are good spenders.

Today with the advance of technology it is challenging to lock out savings, especially in an era where you can make deposits and withdrawal on your mobile phone. The truth is that where there is a will, there is always a way. You can still lock out funds today by investing in term deposits accounts for periods of over one year. You can also buy Treasury bills or Federal bonds that could run for years. You can invest in private equity funds or long-term mutual funds.

I will give you a crude but relevant illustration. I had a friend who was not educated but was shrewd and street smart. He was a hard-working trader. Once, I asked him how he knew he was making money. He laughed. He told me he knows exactly how much profit he makes annually. He owed no bank and owed nobody. Nobody owed him. He sold and bought in cash. At the end of the year he would calculate the cost price of all of his unsold inventory and add it to cash in the bank. That's what traders call "stock taking." Because he carried out a similar exercise the previous December, the difference between the balances of both year-ends represents the profit or loss made in the year. For example, if inventory and cash was $300,000 as of the preceding December 31 and at the following December 31, cash and inventory totals $450,000, that implied that his profit after all expenses is $150,000. As crude as this calculation is, it is in line with accounting principles and is called a change in net worth. If there is no equity injection, the key thing that leads to change in net worth is retained earnings or undistributed profit.

The lesson that I learnt from this trader is that he would immediately take out that $150,000 and invest it in real estate. This way he successfully locked out the surplus income and preserved his wealth. This businessman may not have attended any of the Ivy League business schools, but he is wealthy by common sense. Let's learn from him.

8. GET UPDATED AND GET INFORMATION

Corporations often set up and fund research and development (R&D) departments. The objective is to constantly research and develop new products. R&D gathers information on what rivals and peers are doing. Intelligence gathering is part of their assignment. With this structure, corporations get contemporary information relevant for decision making. They monitor performances of their products and report to management. They monitor activities of peers and rivals. They develop new products to constantly meet the needs of their consumers. They are informed, and there are no surprises.

If you want to preserve your wealth, you need to be up to date on issues concerning your business. You need to know what peers are doing. You need to know about new products and new ways of doing things. If you don't catch up with the fast-changing business environment, you will be left behind. You need to understand economic issues such as gross domestic product, inflation, etc. You could lose your wealth if you make investment decisions based on stale or incomplete information.

CHAPTER 6

HELLO, CEO

Every company is led by a chief executive officer (CEO). The CEO is possibly the most important person in the corporation. The buck stops at his or her table because that person oversees every aspect of the corporation's operations including finance, production, marketing, and human resource management. That individual is the key decision maker and has to liaise with the board of directors to push the agenda of the corporation through. That person has to liaise with staff to ensure board decisions are implemented. Overall, the CEO's job is to ensure value creation is achieved for the shareholders and to ensure the corporation does not go bust or into excessive debt while ensuring that decent dividends are paid. In general, the CEO has to ensure financial stability for the corporation.

Guess what? You are the CEO of your personal "corporation." You are the CEO of your family. You are the CEO of your career. You are the one making decisions about your life, and you are the product of all the decisions you have made to date. Your future will depend a lot on the decisions you make today. The CEO of a company gets fired for losing money by making terrible mistakes in decision making. Stop blaming others for what happens to you. Start taking responsibility. The actions you take or decline to take have consequences. That's why you must know you are in charge and act accordingly.

In this chapter, we shall review the functions of a corporation's CEO. You will be amazed that they are applicable to you. If you act as the CEO of your personal career/job, and you operate effectively, you will be free from personal financial bondage. Here are some illustrations.

1. STRATEGIC PLANNING

Every CEO is responsible for strategic planning. It's the responsibility of the CEO to plan for the long-term solvency and profitability of the organizations. Part of strategic planning is to focus on production facilities, market share, succession planning, etc. The CEO needs to envision what the future will look like in years to come and needs to plan the resources that must be put together to actualize that vision. He needs to even consider potential changes in the macroeconomic space and anticipate changes in demand and various dynamics including technology. He needs to anticipate potential consumer tastes and even the competitors' potential next steps. It's a deliberate set of objectives, action steps, and expected results.

Do you undertake strategic planning for yourself? Many folks don't. They think it's for corporations only. Let's assume you adopt a child after your fifty-second birthday; it's important you don't throw strategic planning to the winds. That baby will only be eighteen and getting ready to attend college when you are seventy. Who will train her in college? Let's assume you have two children after you married late at forty. Your first baby arrived at forty-one. Your second baby arrived at forty-four. You celebrated the fact that despite your age your babies are great, and I celebrate with you too. But at sixty-five when you retire, your first child will be twenty-five. Hopefully you will be able to see her through college. How about your second baby? She will only be twenty-one when you retire at sixty-five. How do you see her through college, and more especially if she is in medical school?

Let me show you another dimension of personal strategic planning. Let's assume you took your first loan at thirty-eight and got a thirty-year mortgage. You really loved the deal. It was easy to pay. Let's assume you had no professional "accident." You were never fired from work, and your job was stable. Let's assume you keep working until retirement. When you retire at sixty-five you will still have three unpaid years on your mortgage. You need to consider how you intend to pay it. Is your pension large enough to accommodate the mortgage?

Let us look at another aspect of mortgage planning. When you are young and newly married you possibly could make do with a small two-bedroom apartment. You could even live in a studio flat. Over time you had three beautiful children. Naturally you will need a bigger house. And so you and your spouse made a down payment for a five-bedroom home. That's a smart idea. It's a lovely home with a guest room where your children's friends could sleep over on weekends. The home is bubbling and sometimes is noisy. You actually labeled the rooms: boys' room, girls' room, etc. In less than eighteen years, the boys become men, and the girls become ladies.

In a few years' time they begin to leave for college. Just before you can say Jack Robinson, they graduate and get their degrees. They get their homes. Gradually they hardly come home. What used to be "our home" becomes mommy and daddy's home. If they quickly had their babies, your home suddenly becomes grandma or grandpa's home. You still call your wife sweetie. You are in your early fifties. But they call you grandparents.

At this age you will observe that your five-bedroom house is no longer economically sensible. Why should you be paying a mortgage on a five-bedroom home when you and your wife share only one room? Why should you be paying for four rooms that nobody occupies? But you knew twenty years ago that scenario must play out. Did you plan for it? At this point in your life it makes sense to get a smaller house. You could sell the first house. The equity on that house may be enough to fetch you a debt-free smaller home. Even if it's not enough, the monthly mortgage may be very much lower and easier to absorb. The future will always come. Plan for it now.

What about cars? You obviously need a minivan if you have a large young family. You may need a seven-seater four-wheel-drive. When the children get to eighteen years old and have their small first cars, you no longer require that minivan. So why buy a seven-seater vehicle when your only child is already fifteen? It makes sense to always think of the future when planning and making financial decisions.

This same illustration applies to marriages. When I see elderly men marry very young women I know it's a time bomb that may lead to divorce. The truth is the flame of love burns so intensely that it may be difficult to engage in strategic planning. For example, if a forty-eight-year-old man marries a twenty-three-year-old woman, it's a potential crisis. Twenty-two years later, the man would be seventy while the lady would still be a sweet forty-five-year-old ready to rock life. But the bones of the seventy-year-old husband are weak, and he would lack the energy and the drive to sustain the relationship. Taking a walk in the park may not even be easy for the man. While the man is retired, the lady would still be very active in her career. Discussions are no longer aligned, and the man becomes lonely at home. When the father visits the children, their friends ask if that was their grandpa. Suddenly the lady is not too proud to walk around holding hands with her hubby. Unless God intervenes, such marriages ultimately fail. Such failures are a result of failure of strategic planning.

2. STAFFING

Every CEO is careful in hiring staff, especially the key management, and would also need to optimize personnel to ensure the company is neither overstaffed nor understaffed. In addition to hiring, the CEO also ensures regular supervision and training. Among other roles, the CEO must ensure that staffers are motivated while putting structures in place to ensure that they do not incur expenses that could jeopardize the corporation's finances.

I have news for you. You have staff that you manage too. Your "staff" includes your spouse, children, and home attendants. Any of them can run you out of business and push you into debt. Therefore, you need to begin to operate as a CEO in your home. If the corporate CEO will carefully scrutinize his management staff before he hires them, you cannot do less. Your spouse is a codirector in the home. You must carefully choose your spouse. During courtship, the character of your potential spouse will show.

My wife and I have been married for over twenty-seven years. One day during courtship she visited me. I desired to give her a treat and drove her to a shopping center. I told her to buy whatever she desired on my account. To my shock, she purchased only one minor item with a value of less than ten dollars. I took note that I was about to marry a very prudent lady. I've not been proved wrong to date. Practically everything we own today is as a result of her prudence and wise counsel. She always restrained me from frivolous expenses.

I am sure you have heard many stories of spouses that mess up the credit history of their spouses. A number of people are in debt today because their partners are spendthrifts using their credit and debit cards with little or no restraint. If you are not yet married, choose your spouse carefully. If you are already married, seek professional counsel to assist in restraining the guilty party.

How about other "staff," who may be your children? Younger children want to buy the whole world if they can. If they have access to the internet they can place orders of payments on delivery. I know a family that had financial problems because their child kept ordering for movies online, and bills kept arriving by post. Young adults love fashion and love to buy anything that is in vogue. They don't count the costs. Please teach your children how not to waste money. Teach them how to save. If they are still very young, buy them piggy banks. Teach them financial prudence and contentment.

The greatest problem as a young adult is peer pressure. Teach them that families differ and that everyone must live according to what is affordable.

The first English word my wife learned from her father was *contentment*. Accordingly, the first English word my wife taught our lovely children is *contentment*. Children don't know much, no matter how they pretend to know. You are the CEO. Teach them and guide them. Take time to explain the family finances and priorities to them. Run an open system. They may resist initially, but they will ultimately understand.

How about other "staff" who are not your children? These may be relations or friends living with you and attendants such as stewards, chauffeurs, or security personnel. Apply the same principle. Everyone in your home should know that their lifestyle must not create unnecessary debts for you. For example, they must be prudent with the use of water and electricity. Let them know it doesn't make sense to put on the air conditioners during summer only to step outside for hours. The bill will come ultimately. Watch the lifestyles of those living with you. They can push you into the debt trap unwittingly.

Furthermore, as the CEO, sets control mechanisms in place to check excesses. Corporations place monthly limits on certain staff expenses. Set limits for expenses in your home too. Get agreement from everyone and then monitor them. This way you will avoid unpleasant surprises.

Finally, the CEO is careful in the number of staff he hires. The biggest expense item in the family budget profile is the cost of raising a child. From pregnancy until college that child is your financial responsibility. You must therefore carefully plan the number of children you want to have in agreement with your spouse. You must estimate your income level and plan for your children's upkeep. It is unfair to have children you cannot care for. If you are challenged in this area, you could easily enter the debt trap. Please exercise caution. It's within your control. If you have already made the mistake, counsel your children not to repeat similar mistakes.

Family meetings should be held regularly at the dining table. Share information with your family. Let everyone know what everyone else is doing. Openly correct excesses with love. There should be no hidden agenda or pretenses. Let the family budget be discussed. Let family challenges be disclosed. When I had financial challenges and an overbearing mortgage, I called my children and shared with them. I told them everything. The children understood why certain expenses could not be incurred. No child will request holiday trips if you have openly shared what you are going through. Don't hide your challenges. You may even get suggestions from the children that may be invaluable. I have found my children's counsel amazingly invaluable. Keep communicating with all internal stakeholders.

3. PERIODIC PERFORMANCE REVIEW

Every CEO conducts periodic performance reviews. Some do it monthly, and it's called a monthly performance review (MPR). When done quarterly it's called the quarterly performance review (QPR). It's basically performance tracking.

The essence of the periodic review is to ensure among other things that revenue budgets are being met. It also checks to ensure that expense limits are not exceeded. In addition, key projects earmarked for implementation are reviewed to ensure that they are on track.

Do you periodically review your expenses? Do you even have personal budgets? Do you have a monthly review to check how much you spend on gas, feeding, clothing, transportation, etc.? Do you maintain records? Have you ever asked your bank to send your statements of accounts to enable your review to ensure there are no errors? Some people think that banks are spirits and can never make mistakes. I have worked for over thirty-two years in banking and financial consultancy, and the fact is that banks can and do make mistakes. Therefore, it makes sense to request your bank statements and verify their correctness and accuracy.

Separate the items into expenses and income and then review all expenses including the bank charges. Review your bank check stubs and compare the statement entries with the stubs. If you have made payments/withdrawals using electronic facilities such as ATMs, mobile phones, or internet-enabled devices such as your tablets and computers, you will obviously not have paper check stubs for such. You don't have to worry. Remember that every time you use your card in a store or make internet transactions, you receive mobile phone alerts from your bank. If you don't have one set up already, you can request this from your bank for a minimal fee. In the same vein, you get emails from your bank each time you deposit money or make a withdrawal. Don't delete such mails until the month ends. They will come in handy.

Compare the bank emails/mobile phone alerts with the statements from the bank. Report to your bank if you find strange or incorrect entries. Raise an alarm early, and the bank will correct them.

This regular monthly review and reconciliation will help you keep a lid on your expenses and help you refrain from abnormal unplanned expenses. Once you notice that you have exceeded your monthly limit, you may take corrective actions immediately. One of such actions may be to cut down your expenses in the following month. You need this tracking and monitoring discipline in order to end the year without an unexpected debt.

In addition, you need to track revenue targets. You must have listed your various revenue sources and amounts on a monthly basis. Obviously your salaries will be a major source of revenue. If you have other investments such as real estate and marketable securities, they can be veritable revenue sources. Please review the bank statements to also ensure that the credit entries agree with what you expect.

After that, be sure that it's not too far off from your budget. If you have substantial adverse variances, then you should be concerned. If your revenue has declined, you must cut down your expenses further in the following month in order to have a clean budget and escape debts. It's the old saying: cut your coat according to your clothes (no more according to your size). You must never have an aggressive expenditure lifestyle if your revenue profile is not bullish or aggressive.

Finally, at the beginning of each year the CEO submits a budget to the board of directors for review and approval. The annual budget is split into twelve months to track performance.

Do you also have an annual/monthly personal budget? At the beginning of the year, people make New Year's resolutions. Some forget them within the first two weeks of the new year. It should not be so for you. The secret is to write down your budget. Write down your monthly planned revenues and accompanying expenses. Follow it through. It's a deliberate, thought-out plan. An unplanned budget cannot be monitored. As the saying goes: if you fail to plan, you have planned to fail. Start planning your financial life. Start monitoring it too. Take corrective measures early. This way you will avoid the debt trap.

4. MARKETING/PUBLIC RELATIONS

The CEO is the chief image maker and the face of the corporation. That individual maintains direct relationships with key external stakeholders, top community leaders and top government agencies, other CEOs of comparable standing, and strategic key suppliers. The CEO may even organize end of year appreciation dinners and other relevant functions to relate with key stakeholders. The CEO is the brand and promotes the brand.

As a CEO who do you relate with? How well do people know you in your community? Are you respected? Is your family a good brand? Can people trust your family's brand name? Is your family name associated with vices or virtues? How much goodwill does your family have?

How much people respect you will determine how much trust they place in you. Trust could determine how much favor you can elicit from the community. That could determine the level of cooperation and concessions you can receive. If your family brand is tarnished, you will be forced to work alone. You will always have your back against the wall. It's expensive in life trying to make it alone, as no man is an island.

Let me give you an example. When I was studying for my professional accountancy examinations, a friendly neighbor who was already certified lent me his books. That saved me money. At the same time my boss granted me unusual extended off days from my office to enable me to prepare for the exams. She even visited me at home to encourage me to study more. I became a chartered/certified accountant by spending far less and earning much more. It was a matter of good relations with neighbors and associates. Create a good image of yourself.

Many people have business breakthroughs or high-paying jobs based on a recommendation by associates or friends. You never know who knows someone that knows someone. The world is very small. It's a global village. Be friendly to your neighbors. Relate easily with others. Be the chief image maker of your life. Nobody can market you more than you can market yourself. Do it, save money, and boost your revenues.

5. INTERNAL COMMUNICATIONS

The CEO of a corporation communicates with internal staff, calls regular management meetings to review operations, attends board meetings to give accounts to the board of directors, and attends occasional general staff meetings to speak to staff at least once a year. In between these scheduled meetings, the CEO also communicates by writing. He writes to the board providing detailed reports or seeking approvals. He sends circulars to staff from time to time giving guidelines and directives.

How do you operate? The management in your home is your spouse. Management meetings are held regularly in corporations. How often do you meet with your spouse? Do you have separate rooms? Do you go out for evening walks? Do you talk regularly while at work? Do you have dinner together? How often do you talk and plan your family income and expenditure? Most embarrassing family expenses arise because couples are not bonded. They live together physically without unity of purpose because they don't talk as much as they should. Couples make assumptions. How many times have you seen couples return from different grocery stores carrying similar items? Each person went shopping without talking to the other, and they end up wasting money by duplicating purchases.

Even more expensive is the potential of divorce arising from poor communication and misunderstanding. Spouses should not live by conjectures. As in corporations, where there is poor communication the rumor mill takes over. How about communicating with your children?

In order to achieve unity of purpose and eliminate potentially problematic financial issues, there must be free flow of information within the family unit. There must be shared visions. There must be open budgets. There must be discussions on key expenditures and plans that will ultimately lead to financial costs. Couples must meet formally and informally in the bedroom and in the living room.

Family dinner with open discussions should be encouraged. This way you eliminate unpleasant surprises that could degenerate into financial crises. Whether we like it or not, every plan—be it personal or group— will ultimately have financial implications. Open, frank, and free discussions at the family level will obviously assist in securing the best options available that will be supported comfortably with the financial resources of the family.

CHAPTER 7

THE POWER OF EDUCATION

Education is a critical key to escaping financial bondage. Sound education liberates the mind and enables you to make quality decisions that will surely help you avoid financial bondage. In addition, quality education empowers you to be at your professional best so that your income levels are substantially enhanced. Here are some relevant issues concerning education.

1. COLLEGE EDUCATION

Those that acquire a minimum of an undergraduate degree from a good university are likely to cross over the poverty line. They are likely to be in the middle class, escape financial bondage, and secure well-paying jobs, especially if they are financially disciplined. Their chances for prosperity will be higher if they obtain a second degree, and the chances will be better still if the degree is from an Ivy League university.

It's not a luxury to pursue a university degree. It's a necessity to graduate into the middle class. I know it's expensive, but you must attach the same importance to obtaining a university degree as securing a home or buying the car you love. If you can take a home loan to buy a house, you can take a loan to pay for your university education. It will pay off later.

My father and I secured a personal loan for my college degree, and I paid it off a few years after graduation. The fact also is that there are grants, scholarships, and all forms of student aids available in many universities for bright and smart students. My daughter has benefited from one. I have benefited from another. If you're ready to work hard, there will always be someone somewhere ready to assist you. Start first. Stop being timid. Believe you can do it. Begin to dream big and have great visions. Write down your visions. Pursue the visions. You will ultimately achieve that vision.

I have a potentially controversial bit of advice. After you have obtained your degree, please ensure you also marry someone with a college degree. The English have a saying that birds of a feather flock together. There is also an expression that says iron sharpens iron. You need to marry someone who will be at the same level of understanding and reasoning with you. You need to live with someone who will not pull you down financially. You need a spouse who will add to what you have already. When both of you pool your resources together, you are likely to experience financial freedom.

2. CAREER PLANNING

You should be careful in making career choices. First you must choose a career that you love dearly. You are likely to be fulfilled and creative in a career you love. Your career is that one you would choose, even if you are not paid for it. You are likely to be ingenious in that career and create new products that will make you rich.

I applied to medical school after high school, but today I am deeply grateful that I am not a doctor. I would have been a disastrous doctor, as I am not essentially a patient person. I don't have the attributes of a typical doctor, but I applied because my friends were applying. We loved the glory and honor that goes with the profession. It was a guidance and counseling teacher in high school who noted my natural aptitude and encouraged me to withdraw my application to medical school. He asked me to apply to study finance. That was forty years ago. Today I am deeply grateful that I received that counsel.

Another issue about career choice is competence. What are you capable of studying? Many people have enrolled into programs where they lack relevant competencies. Why should you enroll into the engineering if you are not good in mathematics? Why should you apply to medical school if you are not comfortable with sciences? God has given everyone a gift. Gravitate toward your area of natural gifting. You are likely to excel in that profession and make money.

Yet another issue in career planning has to do with the changing needs of the economy. The economy evolves. Find out where there is need at the moment and pursue careers toward that area. A close family friend is an information technology (IT) expert. He is already making tons of money in IT. Recently and despite his success on the job, he left his full-time job and returned to the university to study anticybercrime technologies and robotics. He believes this area holds new opportunities and has few professionals.

Today there are a lot of opportunities in science, technology, engineering, and mathematics (STEM). Focus on that if you have the competence. There is a scarcity of medical professionals (doctors, dentists, nurses, radiologists, ophthalmologists etc.). If you have the competence, why not study any of those professions? You can make yourself relevant to your country without making yourself indispensable. If you have what is required, those who require you will come looking for you. Then you will make good money and escape the debt trap.

3. CONTINUOUS PROFESSIONAL EDUCATION

Education can get stale if you don't update it. No matter your level of certification in your profession, you must realize that you need continuous improvement. In some professions like mine, we call it mandatory continuous professional education. New laws can come into operation. New systems and procedures are constantly being developed. New facilities and technologies to aid professional practice are always being developed. New operating standards, guidelines, and policies are being issued by regulatory agencies and professional association boards.

Unfortunately, some people ignore the need to update themselves. Some just manage to get the barest minimum education required to remain in practice. The world is moving very fast, and changes are happening almost on a daily basis, especially with the support of technology. Many people who have been left behind have lost clients and ultimately revenue. Some others who need to apply new technology have lost the advantage of cost savings as they stick to their old way of doing things. Change is a constant. Develop an open mind to constantly improve by applying the most modern and most efficient tools and facilities.

4. BROADER KNOWLEDGE

I am happy that you are reading this book even though you may not be a finance specialist. This is one step toward broadening your knowledge. I feel unhappy when I see professionals who know absolutely nothing about other professions that affect their daily lives. Some people will never watch business or economic news on television while others don't understand basic economic terms such as inflation, gross domestic product, and foreign exchange rates. Some don't care about job reports. But all these are vital statistics that economists use to measure the health of the economy. You are part of the economy. If the economy is passing through a depression or recession, it will ultimately affect everyone including you. In the same way that you will want to know from the doctor your blood sugar level, blood pressure level, or your pulse, you need to know the health of the economy from time to time.

How about knowledge that is not related to the economy? You need that too. If you need advice of an attorney it's reasonable that you have basic knowledge of the law. Recently a member of my church committed a major traffic offense. None of us knew the maximum penalty for such offenses. We were completely ignorant of the law. We were so confident that the highest penalty would be a monetary fine or suspension of his driving license. To our utter amazement, when the case was called up in court, the judge ruled that the vehicle be forfeited to the state. It was in the law. We did not know the basic laws that affect our daily lives.

Before you meet your doctor, obtain some knowledge about general well-being. This way you can have meaningful discussions with your doctor and ask relevant questions. If you need to build a house, obtain some knowledge of issues concerning construction including architectural drawings, building materials, or real estate. It's easy for a construction personality to sell you a project or proposal that could make you lose money if you have no idea about the real estate industry. If you have some basic knowledge, you can negotiate better and save money. If you know what is wrong with your vehicle, you can negotiate better with your mechanic. If you understand basic stock market issues, you can negotiate better with your stockbroker. If you have basic knowledge of any profession, you increase your negotiation capability and obviously save money by cutting costs. That's how to maximize personal value and escape the debt trap. Enlarge your knowledge base and broaden your understanding of issues around you.

5. MENTORING

Nobody knows it all. Nonetheless, the people who are more experienced in your profession have a lot to teach. Every profession has deep unwritten secrets, and the more experienced professionals have the secrets.

After you have acquired formal academic education, ensure you get on-the-job professional education. It's a bit informal and you acquire it by observing the veterans. They can guide you and mentor you. It's been proven that when someone is properly mentored, the person will most likely turn out to be better than his mentor. The reason is simple. The mentee learns from the mistakes of the mentor and tries to avoid such errors. This way the error rates of the mentee are less.

Another benefit of having a mentor is the need to be exposed to clients. This is often very critical for personal professional practices such as defense attorneys, tax consultancy, financial audits, stockbrokers, and real estate agencies. The essence of such tutelage is that you could be exposed to a broad range of clients and can end up forming a great personal relationship with some of them. When you eventually set up your own personal practice, your initial set of clients may be formed from the clients you met in the office of your mentor. This way you take off with a bang and push your revenue upward rapidly. Don't be in a hurry to take off. Attending college and getting a degree is great. But informal education under a mentor prepares you better for the real world after your formal education. You are smart if you don't repeat someone else's mistakes of the past. Learn from them.

CHAPTER 8

YOUR ATTITUDE AND DEBT FREEDOM

Attitude plays a key role in making an exit from debt bondage. Living debt free involves battles. The battles are fought and won in the mind. Your thought process and mind-set will influence your actions. Your thoughts and attitudes are the invisible software that drives the hardware of living debt free. As a man thinks in his mind, so he is. You must therefore guard your heart because everything you will do or not do flows from there. Here are some of the issues of life that are determined by matters of the heart that would enable you to live debt free.

1. MAKING CHOICES

There is good and evil in the world. If you do good, you will walk free. If you do evil, you will most likely end up in prison. In the same vein, if you make certain decisions in life you will be debt free. If you make some other decisions, you will be in debt bondage. The amazing thing about what you do or do not do is dependent on your choices. Nobody makes choices for you. What you are today is a product of the various choices you have made in the past. What you will be in the future will be determined by the choices you make today.

Let me illustrate with a personal example. As a young man I hated poverty. I was born into poverty, and poverty surrounded me. I made a choice from a young age to exit poverty. As a young boy in junior high school, I admired a distant uncle of mine. He had attended the University of Colombia and at that time worked for Chase Manhattan Bank. He was a middle class person evidently. I loved his well-starched and ironed shirts. I looked forward to being like him when I grew up. I approached him. I told him I admired him. I asked him to advise me of the subjects I should major in while still in high school to enable me be like him when I grow up. He advised me to focus more on mathematics and economics. I ended up studying finance in the university.

I later served as a young accounts manager in a small private company. And then I had an option to take up a temporary job with a lower salary in a subsidiary of Chase Manhattan Bank. I made a choice to take the lower-paying job in order to help me make a career in banking. It was through the assistance of the same uncle that I secured the banking job in the Chase subsidiary. These were deliberate choices.

While I was working in the bank I made yet another choice. I chose to become a chartered/certified accountant. I knew the consequences. I knew the price. It had financial implications. I knew it would shut me out of the social scene for about three years. I made the choice. Today I look back and remain grateful that I made those hard choices. Make your choices with the future you in mind.

2. CULTURE OF EXCELLENCE

Excellence sets you apart from the crowd. With excellence, instead of being in the "crowd," you will be in the "cloud." Excellence lifts you up. Excellence produces premium quality. Premium quality commands premium compensation. Whatever you do, do it very well. Everyone likes good premium value. But it takes special craftsmanship to produce special products.

Excellence includes timeliness. Time is money. Deliver your services/products at the time agreed upon. If possible deliver ahead of time. When I joined the subsidiary of Chase Manhattan Bank, I worked extra hard into weekends to deliver the jobs assigned to me. My bosses took note. It became my culture everywhere I worked. This accelerated my promotions in my banking career. I was already sitting on the board of a commercial bank as a director at the age of forty.

Part of excellence is to deliver nondefective products/services. There should be zero defects on your products. Whatever products you make or services you render is a mirror of you. Nobody likes error-ridden jobs or products with factory defects. Be conscious of the fact that consumers do not have time for explanations or long stories. In any case, there is a competitor next door making a similar product with premium quality at a lower price. You may not find one in your physical neighborhood, but with one click on the internet every shopper has an option. A generation that has grown up is not interested in traditional shopping. They have no time to waste. They are internet savvy. They see the world as their village. They are growing in leaps and bounds daily.

Excellence includes packaging. Excellent delivery and packaging is very important. Excellence includes sourcing raw materials and inputs and putting them through the best production process. It also includes the best-quality staff, consistent quality control, and a hygienic environment. Your products may be for a local market, but they must meet global standards because your competition is international. This way you will sell more and make more money.

3. INTEGRITY

Literally every day, genuine businessmen and businesswomen are shopping for partners and associates all over the world. Many suppliers of various products are in constant search of agents, distributors, and joint venture partners. The only unfortunate thing is that men of integrity are in short supply. I always tell people when I speak to audiences that capital is not scarce. They marvel when I say this. The bank's vaults are overflowing with money, and banks do not make money until they lend out the money in their vaults. Banks are shopping for men and women of integrity who have good business ideas they can finance. Banks actually engage in marketing for good borrowing clients. There are private equity investors with billions of dollars searching for men of integrity who will partner with them. Subject to local regulatory constraints, banks would love to lend money without collateral. To a bank, integrity—or character—is the strongest driving force in determining whether to lend or not. Many manufacturers could have enjoyed cheap and longer-term supplier's credits if they were men of integrity.

Integrity engenders trust. When other people trust you, access to cheaper financing becomes a norm. If capital is abundantly available to you at a reasonable comparative rate, your cost of doing business will be lowered, and profit margins will increase. Mark my word. It's difficult to find a person of integrity in the debt trap, especially if that individual is ready to work hard.

4. HARD WORK

Hard work is indispensable for success. I have taken time to study successful people. I have studied successful sportsmen. They always spend extra time practicing long after the others have gone to rest. I've studied successful entertainers. They practice a lot into the nights. I've studied wealthy businessmen. They don't waste their time on trivialities. They work hard and often into their nights. They also consciously hire those that work very hard. I have studied successful preachers. They stay awake most nights. I have never seen a successful person who is lazy. There are none anywhere in the world.

On the other hand, laziness guarantees poverty and entry into the debt trap. Whenever I make speeches I tell my audience that the entertainers/ sportsmen they watch on television all day do not even know those guys who watch them. They get paid big bucks while you spend the whole day watching them and refusing to work. They spend their nights working. If you spend your nights sleeping and your days watching television and movies, how do you intend to exit the debt trap?

Stop looking up to governments or anyone else to feed and house you. You are not being fair on those that are working if you look forward to government feeding and caring for you. Why should the government provide for the needs of your children when the government did not give birth to those children? You did. And you knew it would cost money to care for them before they were born. I have no problems if you decide to have ten children. But please be sure you will work hard enough to meet all their needs until they become legal adults.

Has it occurred to you that if everyone works very hard our collective productivity would be extremely high, and we would have enough to spare for the future? Unless you are sick, there is no excuse acceptable for not working hard. If the wealthy are still working hard, why should the poor stop working?

Get up and work. Engage in extra work. Ordinary work will produce ordinary results. Extraordinary work will produce extraordinary results.

5. FEAR NOT

Someone said that no does not mean rejection, but that it means "next opportunity." You must overcome fear if you want to succeed and escape the debt trap. When you fall, nobody should mock you because you know you will rise again. Fear of failure is not in the books of those who are successful. Thomas Edison was said to have been involved in over one thousand experiments before he discovered the incandescent light we use today called electricity. It was said that at a point in time his laboratory in New Jersey got razed to the ground as a result of his experiments. He refused to give up.

If you are afraid that you will fail, you are most likely to fail. If you don't even make an attempt because of fear, you have already failed.

Deal with the fear factor. It's in the mind. Failing on an assignment does not make you a failure. You just need to try again. You need to keep trying until you succeed. Stop living in the agony of the past. Stop living in the pains and regrets of the past. It's a new day. A new day presents opportunities for a new beginning. There is nobody who has succeeded that has never failed before. We accountants have an account we call profit and loss account. It's one account that has profits (successes) and losses (failures) in one statement. Overcome fear. Get up and try again.

6. FOCUS

In life there will always be many things competing for your time. It's impossible to do all of them at the same time. You must therefore prioritize. You must clearly determine which one can wait and which one must be done right away.

A lady in college fell in love with another student. She became pregnant, and they got married. She never completed college degree, but her lover graduated. Unfortunately, they later divorced. Her husband escaped the debt trap, but she didn't.

I will tell you another story. Becoming a certified/chartered public accountant requires a lot of discipline. It will cost you a lot in finances and time. It will keep you out of the social scene for two to three years. You will definitely give up quite a lot, but when you become certified, you can be sure plum jobs will be readily available.

Thirty-two years ago I was determined to become a certified accountant. I was clearly focused. I knew what I wanted. But then I was in a relationship that was potentially leading to marriage. I was working in a bank and also attending accounting lectures from 6:00 p.m. to 9:00 p.m. daily on working days. On Saturdays and Sundays, I attended such lectures from 8:00 a.m. to 5:00 p.m. Many times we slept over in the classrooms. We studied late into the nights. My fiancée kept coming to my apartment on weekends without meeting me. She kept complaining; I kept explaining.

My explanations made no sense to her. I was clearly focused, and I knew where I was going. I was ready to sacrifice my time to excel in the future. She dropped off. I did not mind even though I was hurt. However, because I had a clear singular purpose, I pursued my ambition. I actualized it. I am glad that two years later, I became a chartered accountant, and I changed jobs. Two years after that I met my wife.

Everything works together for good. Remain focused. There will always be "majors" and "minors." Major on the "majors." Some things can wait. Some other things cannot wait. Pursue those things that cannot wait now. Leave the issues that can wait. You will always handle them in the future

7. DETERMINATION: FIGHT THAT BATTLE

I am sure you have heard of the expression "Winners never quit." In your battle to escape the debt trap, you will face many battles. There will be many enticing options to quit. You will be discouraged many times. Those who lose their battles will advise you to forget the battle. Choosing the way out will only guarantee your entry into the bondage of debt. Fighting your way through will enable your escape.

I could have quit college, but I chose not to. My father (may God bless his soul) and I fought it through by going to borrow money from a relation for the tuition. I personally signed to pay the loans upon graduation. I did pay. I visited a good old friend to borrow money from to support the expensive cost of becoming a professional accountant. He was a successful businessman. He kept giving me appointments to discuss the loan but never kept them. One day I visited again, and one of his workers called me aside. He confided in me that his boss had said I was wasting my time and that he would never give me a loan. He expected that I would give up after many disappointments. I stopped trying to see him. I faced some other friends. Eventually I got enough for the examinations. Today, as they say, the rest is history. It's all about determination. It's all about willingness to fight it through.

There is no easy way to success. Natural forces may be the opposition. Friends may oppose you. Relations may be the source of obstruction. Colleagues in the office may oppose you. It may be financial or marital limitations or even spiritual obstructions. The enemy may pit you against yourself. My only advice is to be determined to win. Never give up. Expect battles. Prepare for war. Fight the battles. Never surrender. Make up your mind that it will never be over until you are declared the winner. Don't ever forget that if there are no battles to fight, everyone will be successful. Don't ever forget that the forces that kept you in debt bondage are strong forces. They will fight to keep you there. You must overpower them by doing the right tough things. You must overpower them by getting a good education no matter the cost. Good education may be expensive, but as the saying goes, "If you think education is expensive, try ignorance."

I know you will win at the end.

8. DELEGATION

One age-old economic principle is called division of labor. It still works. It simply means that jobs are assigned to different people according to their competencies. This way the boss coordinates and gets a better result. This way there is specialization and costs come down because there are fewer defective products while the overall organization objectives are met and even surpassed.

The principle of delegation flows from division of labor. Delegation simply implies the boss cannot do everything.

You need to delegate in your home if you need to save money and be more productive. However, for you to effectively delegate you need to understand the core competencies of everyone in the home. For example, although I understand and practice investment, my wife is a better saver. She is extremely prudent. She can haggle and bargain to the last cent. Believe me I consult her on savings. She handles quite a lot. With her there is no wastage and, you must justify what went wrong with an old product for you to replace it. I trust her with savings.

Again, my wife is good with construction-related issues. She can literally design and construct a home from start to finish. She can argue constructively with architects, builders, carpenters, plumbers, electricians etc. She can guide them. When they disagree with her, they always regret it because at the end they find her arguments to be true. The amazing thing is that my wife is a sociologist. But construction flows in her veins. I hand over all matters about construction to her. She gets the best deals all the time. She saves the family money.

I am sure you know that if you have IT-related issues the best consultant you can get is your teenage son or daughter. Instead of wasting money hiring consultants to fix your software or hardware issues, consult your teenagers for free.

Learn to delegate at home. You cannot do everything by yourself. By so doing you will have more time for your own areas of core competencies, and you will get the best out of everybody while saving money. Delegation at home will create an atmosphere of cooperation, which will engender team spirit. When all these are done efficiently, your family could escape the debt trap.

9. AVOID PROCRASTINATION

Procrastination is postponing to a future date the action you could conveniently carry out today. By deferring the action to a future date, you run many risks. For example, if it's a new product, you run the risk of someone else launching it before you do. Many people would have been extremely rich today if they launched out into the deep the very day they got the vision. The right strategy is to write the vision down, and run with the vision. You don't lie on the bed or sit around with the vision. You don't stand or even walk with the vision. The sure way is to run with the vision.

Why should you run? Time is money. Time waits for nobody. If you don't run with the vision, someone else will run with it.

It took me about four years to get my first book ready for publication. Yet it remained unpublished for three years after it was ready. It was only when I saw a book whose title was close to mine that I literally woke up. We suffer a lot of damage when we procrastinate. Some great ideas never come to fruition when we place them on hibernation mode. Some others come up very expensive due to radical changes in environmental and macroeconomic factors. In some cases, change in laws may arise due to delay. In some other cases technology may change so quickly that the idea becomes obsolete even before it's developed.

If you want to build wealth, do not procrastinate. Opportunities are not available forever. Capture them as they are made available. Every day has its opportunities. The day you miss will never come back. If you want to be successful and exit the debt trap, stop deferring actions. Act on ideas promptly. Stop procrastinating.

10. DEFER GRATIFICATION

There are three major stages in a person's life where that person is capable of making decisions. These are the teenage/youth years, middle age, and finally old age. Your greatest energies are available during the first stage, which spans from about sixteen to forty. This is when you can have three jobs without joint pains or combine your regular job with full-time education. Some people argue that if one does not own his first house within this age bracket it will be a tough task to own a home in middle age. The unfortunate thing, however, is that at this age the lure and temptation for pleasure is at its highest. People who cave in and focus on pleasure may struggle in middle age. The recommendation is to defer self-gratification at this youthful age and make massive investments and build wealth.

Middle age may run from age forty-one to sixty-five. At this point in time your energy levels have started waning. Also expenses increase and can hardly be controlled while your capacity to invest is reduced substantially because of those expenses. For example, at this age the children are most likely in college while you may also be paying a mortgage on your home. Some of these expenses can be quite substantial. Meanwhile, you can no longer hold two or three jobs. That's the time to rely on the investments you made in the youth league.

Finally, old age (sixty-five and beyond) is retirement age. You are likely to be on pensions or volunteering. Your income is very minimal. Depending on how you planned your life, by this time you should not be paying for children's college education. Again, the savings and investments of the youth league will come in handy.

With these in mind, you would need to work extremely hard when you are in the youth league. Make massive savings and investments. These savings will help you pick up your bills in middle age and also help you enjoy your retirement. With these deliberate action steps you will most likely escape the bondage of debt.

11. OBEY THE LAWS (COMPLIANCE ATTITUDE)

It's cheaper to obey the law than to contravene it. In fact, one easy way to be entrapped in debt is to keep running afoul of the law. If you keep on having traffic offenses your insurance company will increase your premium. If you keep drinking and driving you will likely get involved in more motor accidents. Your insurance company knows you are a great risk. Your insurance premium goes up automatically.

Pay your taxes. Pay the correct taxes. All those who think they are smart and try to cheat on taxes always pay a big price at the end. Eventually they would have to pay back taxes and a penalty when caught. Some may even end up in jail.

If you sign a contract, abide by the terms. Don't try to circumvent it. You never know what could happen in the future. When the case comes up in future, the liabilities you tried to avoid will still be awaiting your payment along with penalties. Be law abiding at home, in your community, and in your place of work. It pays to obey the law. Live a life of compliance with regulations and laws. Running afoul of the law is sure to place you in financial difficulties. It may not happen now. But it will surely happen one day in the future.

CHAPTER 9

EXITING THE DEBT TRAP

When a man is in prison he has to convince the judge that he is remorseful of his bad deeds. He has to behave well in prison. That's why prisoners enjoy parole after years of consistent good behavior.

Similarly, it is necessary that you "repent" of the wrong deeds that put you in the debt trap. You must show commitment that you do not intend to continue with the old ways before you are empowered to exit. In most cases all you may be required to do is to reverse whatever put you in the debt bondage. There are, however, some other follow-up actions you may be required to carry out in order to exit the debt trap. Here are some of them.

1. FORGET THE PAST BUT LEARN LESSONS

There is a saying that only a fool will keep on doing the same thing and hope to get a different result. If you continue in the ways that put you in debt, you will not be able to exit the debt trap. The old mistakes must not be repeated. You must resolve within yourself to chart a new course. But you must not dwell in the past. Your mental disposition must change. You must stop blaming yourself. You must tell yourself that the past is gone, but the future looks promising.

I passed through a debt crisis that almost led me into depression. My friends kept encouraging me to forget the past, and I did. That's why I can write about it now. If you don't let the past go, it will be a great burden that can weigh you down. The past can obliterate your vision and prevent you from seeing new opportunities. The past is baggage; throw it into the garbage bin.

Nonetheless do not forget to take lessons from the debt crises. Every mess has a message. You should do a self-evaluation and document them. I have a diary where I documented mine. Part of the lessons I am sharing with you in this book are the records of my journey documented in my diary. You are not likely to repeat a mistake if you document it.

2. EXPLORE NEW OPPORTUNITIES

When your mind is reset to put the past behind you, it will be time to explore new business ideas. It may be a new way to do the same old business or a new business completely.

The beginning point is to understand what your areas of strength are. Believe me you have an area of strength. There is something you are capable of doing that gives you a unique advantage. For example, when I found myself locked up in debt, I also did not have a regular job, and I needed to earn an income. When a regular job was not immediately available, I started teaching. I reached out to training agencies who offered me part-time ad hoc opportunities to teach. Income started rolling in. It was tedious. It was not regular. But it solved a lot of financial problems. Don't bemoan your debt situation. Take actions that will generate cash flows almost immediately.

3. ENGAGE YOUR CREDITORS

When your debt records are in bad shape, don't run away from your creditors. In my three decades of banking and financial consultancy, I have observed that many debtors run into trouble for avoidable reasons.

Many debtors just stay away from their creditors, and this leads to trouble. Banks will always assume that a debtor who refuses to meet with them after the obligation has fallen due is merely daring them. Then the banks will invoke the full weight of the law on the debtor by leveraging on the contract signed.

Banks love engagement. Banks love borrowers who would willingly visit and explain their bad cases. It's preferable to document same. You can secure even more loans if necessary. For example, if you are executing a project, and the existing loan is not sufficient to complete the project, you will most likely default in meeting the obligations. The only solution is for the bank to provide an additional credit line to complete the project. Then hopefully the project begins to generate cash flows to pay back both loans. In some cases, most especially if the default was caused by adverse macroeconomic situations, the bank will restructure the loan. This means that the bank will extend the tenor and possibly lower the interest rate to ease repayment. This will lessen the burden on a periodic basis. In some rare situations the banks could even forgive or write off some portions of the loans if they clearly see that the debtor has shown good behavior in the past and has no reasonable means of payment.

Do not stay away from your creditors. Stay close. Present all the facts to them. Engage them. Meet with your creditors when you are in debt. It says a lot about your character.

4. BE OPEN TO YOUR FAMILY

There is one thing you must never forget. When you are in financial difficulties, most of your friends will leave you. You will be lucky if one or two stick around. Ninety-nine percent of my friends and relatives stopped picking up my calls when I had financial problems. Please do not expect anything else. It's human nature. Do not feel bad about it.

But the reality is that your immediate family will never leave you. You must be open to them. When I lost my job and was also in debt, I called a special family meeting. My children including my youngest child, who was barely four years old, and my wife were in attendance. I narrated everything to them and showed them documents exonerating me from every form of impropriety. I told them that even though my records were impeccable, I had debts to pay, and I had no job. I asked them for suggestions. We prayed family prayers for divine intervention.

With this family meeting came the explanations that our financial lifestyle as a family must change. We all agreed to forgo many luxuries we were used to. We all suffered together.

This way we had peace at home. We avoided undue pressures especially from the children. I remember sharing my diary with them. Today you are reading part of that diary.

5. SEEK SPOUSE SUPPORT

My wife was a great pillar of financial support in times of my financial crisis. She had her small business. What we called a small business became the dominant income source for the family for the years when I had no regular paid job. The family relied on her for most basic needs. She worked extra hard and sometimes had to obtain supplier's credit from her trading partners.

You will never know how much your spouse loves you until you get into a financial problem.

Reach out to your spouse when in debt. Be humble enough to ask for help. He or she will likely extend a helping hand. My wife was like a rock behind me. She not only provided for the family financially, she provided amazing emotional support and counsel. I recall with nostalgia one evening she took me to a restaurant where I used to take her for dinner. After the wonderful dinner the stewards dropped the bill by my side. My wife reached out for the bill. Then she counted the cash and passed it under the table to me. She did not want the waiters to see what was happening. I took the money along with the tip and happily paid the bill. I felt great. My ego, which I thought was badly bruised, bounced back.

Again, because she was in charge of finances, her prudent management skills were on display. She recommended that we disengage some household attendants. We did and saved a lot of money. Thank God for my wife.

6. RELEASE REDUNDANT ASSETS

If you have a piece of property that yields you little or nothing, dispose of it to realize badly needed cash when you are in debt. This will provide needed cash that can assist to ameliorate your financial situation.

When I was in a financial problem the first thing I did was to sell off a small debt-free commercial property I owned. The next thing I did was to sell our family's second car. My wife sold her jewelry. Paying tuition for the children was solved for a period using the resources realized from these assets. There will always be something to sell when you are in a financial problem.

7. LEAN ON SUCCESSFUL ASSOCIATES

As I mentioned earlier in this chapter, many of your friends and associates will disconnect from you when you are in a debt crisis. Many of them will not return your calls, especially when they observe that you could be a financial burden on them. However, you must make maximum use of the few people that remain close.

In my dire debt period, I approached my former boss. I visited her and narrated all I was passing through. She had a training firm for bankers. She immediately invited me to join her but not as an employee. It was to be on a joint venture basis. If I secured training jobs, we would share profits. If she secured, I would be given the option to serve as a trainer and be paid like any other trainer. This opportunity opened up a source of income to me. My boss, Aunty Mo, became a great blessing. Not only was she paying for my services; she was reaching out to my family. When my daughter secured admission to medical school I was worried, but Auntie Mo immediately gifted us amazing financial support.

In the same period, I offered my personal home to a successful business partner of mine. I was willing to move my family to a smaller apartment so that I could free up cash to pay for my children's education. This rich man amazed me. He picked up some of the education bills himself and declined to purchase my home. Your story may not be exactly like mine. The message is that you should not hide your challenges from your trusted associates who remain close. They may help you financially. They may help you get a job. They may offer you wise counsel that could turn around your situations. Don't stay alone.

8. BE WARY OF NEW DEBT

When a new debt adds to an old debt it may be overwhelming. When you are overwhelmed by debt, you would not be in a good emotional state to handle the debt crisis. If there is a way you can avoid additional debt, by all means please avoid it. If you cannot avoid new debts, make sure that the terms and conditions are flexible and friendly enough.

Let me give an illustration. At the height of my financial crisis, I still had to pay for my children's education. The other option would have been for them to drop out of schools. But that was not an option for me. I approached the school authorities. I explained my financial predicament. They reviewed my records and confirmed that I paid the fees promptly in the past. They saw that we sometimes paid ahead of the due date. They granted me very relaxed and generous payment terms for my children's tuition. We literally paid at our convenience as long as we paid before the end of the academic year. This way we were able to manage to avoid financial embarrassment.

9. MANAGE PERSONAL HEALTH

You need to be in very good health in order to generate income to pay your debt. When a debtor falls critically ill, all sources of income may be on hold. You must therefore manage your health well. Nonetheless, no one can control or predict sickness. You can live well and still fall sick. The most painful thing about debt crisis arises when you don't have medical insurance.

When I lost my job and was in debt, I also lost my medical insurance. This was because my employer provided the medical insurance as part of my benefits on the job. It was therefore highly challenging to handle medical bills when I was in financial crisis. I was admitted into hospital at least twice during this period. I had long hospital stays. The bills were overwhelming. Thank God I had a wonderful doctor who was also my friend. I transferred my medical records to him when I lost my job. He was highly supportive. He offered relaxed terms of payment. Just as with the education bills, my doctor was fantastic. He allowed me to pay whenever I could afford to. He attended to me at all times. Today he remains one of my best friends.

10. HUMBLE YOURSELF

There is a growth principle that is rarely taught in Ivy League business schools. It's the word *humility*. It's a natural law. That law says that if you want to ascend, you must descend first. Some call it stooping to conquer. It says that you first must go down before you get up. You must get ready for what people call menial jobs for you to graduate to white-collar jobs. You must excel on Main Street before you get to Wall Street.

Being in debt crisis is the equivalent of being knocked down. The beginning point is for you to accept that reality. You must therefore humble yourself to pick up any job that you can get. No job is too small for a man that is down. You're not likely to get a plum job at the outset. It's like restarting your career. While you are seeking the good jobs, I assure you that the jobs that will come your way readily would be the kind of jobs you may not like. When I lost my job and was in debt, I first got a job as a teacher. I trained people for some years. Then I got a job as an accountant in a small company. I worked there for less than a year. Then I had to leave to return to my teaching job for another year. Finally, God opened the door for the plum job. Interestingly the experiences I gathered in those small jobs were readily helpful in the plum job.

It's good to aim for the sky. If you arrive at the ceiling, it is fine to start from there. One day you will get to the sky. The truth is that many people who are in debt crisis want their problems to vanish in one night. It does not often work that way. It takes time. Be patient. Be humble. Start small again. Put yourself together gradually. Be consistent. One day you will look back and observe that your financial situation will be turned around. It often takes time to enter into debt. It also takes time to exit from it.

11. AVOID REPEAT ERRORS

One of the greatest mistakes that put me in financial difficulty was overconfidence. I attended some of the best business schools in the United States and England. I believed I was smart. Now I know that I was not as smart as I thought I was. My wife has a master's degree in sociology. She kept telling me to diversify my investments. She loves real estate and construction. She believes you could never get it wrong with real estate. I believed in aggressive income. I believed one could speculate in the capital and money markets in the short run and make quick bucks that could be invested later into hard assets such as real estate.

Then the global economic recession happened. Every stock went tumbling down. The debts I had were covered by 400 percent value of stocks but with the crash I had a massive shortfall. Some creditor banks later took whatever remnants remained of the stocks against the debts of the borrowers. I was one of the beneficiaries, thanks to compassionate creditor banks.

The problem arose because I made grievous investment errors. I refused to take great counsel from my wife. I can assure you that I am completely different today. I know the errors I made. I suffered the consequences of my errors. I am more circumspect than ever in making investment decisions. My question to you is, "Have you learned from the mistakes that put you in debt?" Your mistakes may not be exactly like mine. But you definitely made some mistakes. It may be a lifestyle issue. It's possible you have a penchant for expensive products or that your expenditure profile constantly outweighs your revenue. It's possible that you don't plan your expenses and therefore make purchases on impulse. Whatever is responsible for your mistakes, make amends. If you are not yet in debt, please learn from those that are in debt in order to avoid their mistakes.

12. REMEMBER FORGOTTEN WEALTH

In debt, everything counts. When you are comfortable you can easily scatter your wealth. When you are in debt you have to gather your wealth. Some of that wealth may be forgotten. But you must go looking for your wealth when you are in debt. It may amaze you what you may be able to gather.

Start by taking your pen and paper. You will be amazed how many people have borrowed from you that you have forgotten. You need to collect all your receivables to enable you to discharge your payables.

I know of a lady who was paying money for a time-share facility before she went into debt. She had already paid over 75 percent of the contribution before her debt crisis. She quickly terminated the contract and collected her money back. Someone else had savings in a bank that he had completely forgotten about. It became handy when debt suddenly cropped up.

I know of another man who had some stocks that he had forgotten about. He forgot about it because the investment he made many years ago was very little. What he did not realize was that the stock has benefited from many stock bonuses and splits. Accordingly, the value of the stocks had grown ten times more than the original investment. Someone else had found substantial cash kept away for a long time. I've heard all kinds of amazing testimonies. The secret is to ponder and deeply reflect. You may be surprised what you could put together from "forgotten" assets.

13. GET AN ATTORNEY

You need a friendly attorney by your side when you face a debt crisis. Obviously it will cost a lot to hire a solicitor. But you need one. You never can tell what will happen. You may have a difficult creditor who is not willing to listen to your pleas.

Accordingly, you need an attorney who should be more like a friend and who will provide you with legal counsel and documentation support on friendly payment terms.

I do not recommend that you take legal action against your creditor when you are in debt. It is morally and professionally wrong. It's not acceptable. You should never explore legal loopholes to escape your obligations. You are obligated to pay your debts. Lawyers will tell you that those who come to equity must come with clean hands. However, you must be prepared in case your creditors take legal action against you. In such instances you will have no option but to defend yourself in court. Otherwise stay out of court. Do not shy away from your obligations. Do not operate in deception. Remain honest. Face your challenges with hard work and integrity. Remain positive that you will discharge your debts one day. And you could certainly do so without litigation.

14. NEVER GIVE UP

You may be faced with some frustration and obstacles as you make efforts to exit the debt trap. I assure you that where you expect help to come from may not be where it will eventually come from. Many people will disappoint you, and new projects could fail yet again, while you may be asked to leave a new job that you believed would bail you out. Many people will not want to see you. Doors that previously opened on your first knock may be shut against you.

With these circumstances, you may be tempted to give up. Thoughts of suicide may even come in, and you may be tempted to end it all. Thoughts of filing for bankruptcy may crop up. Some may even suggest divorce.

The truth is that giving up is not an option. Suicide is not an option. It does not pay the debts. The only solution is to be steadfast. The solution is to keep up the fight and remain dogged and positive even in the face of daunting tasks. The only solution is the solution that will ultimately pay the debt. It may take time. The road may be very rough and slippery. The mountains and valleys may be many. But you must be determined to level the mountains and fill up the valleys. You must determine that all the crooked roads must be made straight. If you fall on the slippery roads you must get up and keep trying. One day, on a day like this, if you don't give up, you will be debt free.

CHAPTER 10

FINANCIAL FREEDOM AND THE FUTURE OF CREDIT

Credit is like a revolution. The credit life can only be compared with the technological revolution that has come along with information technology. Credit has completely changed the way we make payments. Clearly many vendors have shown preference for credit cards as against debit cards.

Trade by barter was the earliest means of exchange in medieval ages. Then gold became a means of exchange as central banks maintained gold reserves. Later paper money became popular to replace gold. And recently, banks began to "create" money by issuing credit. Economists now calculate money supply by not only aggregating the currency in circulation but by also adding the money created by commercial banks through credit lines.

In the last thirty decades the money created by banks and merchants has gradually placed printed paper money at the back door. Credit is the new currency. Obviously cash is going to go extinct, as very soon most central banks will not need to print currency notes or mint coins. Just as the gold reserves became unfashionable, so is printed paper money becoming unpopular. Increasingly the demand for cash continues to drastically decline even as the demand for credit increases.

Obviously regulators, tax authorities, statisticians, and various agencies of governments are comfortable with electronic payments because it's easy to track and monitor. That's the right way to go, as it will bring sanity to the financial system.

Businesspeople want to push up their sales so they encourage you to buy a lot now and pay later. Again, that is all right. When we speed up sales, velocity of money is enhanced. Productivity is increased. Gross domestic product is enhanced. More jobs are created. National wealth is enhanced.

Even for the average individual, credit is a blessing when utilized properly. For example, if we all have to save to build our dream homes without credit many people may not complete construction of their homes before they die. If we all have to save before we buy our family cars, many families may never own a car. We cannot escape credit. Credit has come to stay, and credit is good. Credit can only continue to become popular and has the greatest potential of gradually eliminating cash anytime soon.

Here comes the million-dollar question. If the credit culture is like a revolution that no one can stop, how can one avoid being entrapped in debt on a sustainable basis? How do you enjoy benefits of credit without entering into debt bondage? Can you control credit, or is credit controlling you? If your bank pulls the plug (by removing your credit lines) can you survive? Where do you draw the line? How do you really enjoy credit and still maintain control? These are some questions that will be answered in this chapter. The answers will give us a guide on how to live and operate in a credit environment while still enjoying financial freedom on a sustainable basis. Here are some of them.

1. KEEP CASH FLOWS COMING

Here is a fact you must never forget; no matter how much money you have, if you do not continue to earn income, one day whatever you have will be exhausted. You need some level of inflow to counterbalance the inevitable outflows. There are some inevitable outflows such as food and medicine, housing (rent or mortgage), insurance, transportation (car rent or car hire), electricity bills, telephone bills, gas bills, and education bills. I am also assuming that you are not spending your reserves on compulsive outflows such as changing wardrobes and house furniture or going on a vacation.

How quickly your reserves will run out will depend on how much you saved and how much you spend periodically or a combination of both.

If you desire to achieve a sustainable debt-free life you must continue to earn an income. For those who have worked in pensionable organizations, they must earn pension after retirement. If you have made reasonable investments, the inflows will be regularly received in the form of rents and interests. As a young manager I lived very comfortably and could afford holiday trips with my family overseas. The only secret was that I invested my allowances on commercial vehicles that earned me a lot of money daily. Sometimes I earned more money from that source than from my regular paid salary. Today über affords similar opportunities for young people with good cars to augment their regular incomes.

If you want to stay out of debt permanently, your inflows must at least match your outflows. Your cash outflows must not be far ahead of your cash inflows. If that happens, you will be compelled to rely on debt for a long time. If, however, you have healthy cash inflows that surpass or even equal your outflows, you can comfortably use your credit cards knowing that you can easily pay them off.

2. WATCH SPENDING HABITS

No matter how much you earn, your spending habits will determine how much you will have left behind at the end of the pay period. Nobody determines how or when you spend. You are personally responsible for the decisions and consequences of your spending habits. Your spending habits will either heal your finances or harm them.

You alone know what makes you happy. You alone know what you need to purchase to feel like a king. However, I care about one issue: How much are you spending relative to how much you earn? As long as your total expenses far outweigh your total income, there is the danger of landing in debt. Therefore, you need to reorganize your priorities by placing them on a scale of preference. Cut out the least important ones and spend on the most important. Sustainable debt freedom necessitates a strong resolve to manage spending habits.

3. RETAIN YOUR DILIGENCE

There is always a temptation to relax and have fun when people think they have achieved success. The irony of life is that highly successful people never stop working. In fact, many successful people work harder when they have achieved success. I have had rich people say that what drives them to work even harder is the fear of backsliding into poverty. The fact is that it is extremely easy for a rich man to become poor and for a successful person to become a failure.

The moment you stop increasing, you start decreasing. The moment you stop growing, you start shrinking. You must be afraid of sliding into poverty. That must motivate you to keep working hard and exerting profitable energy. Without continued diligence, competitors may take away your market share. Without diligence many macroeconomic factors such as inflation and/or fiscal issues could erode what you think you have kept securely.

Forces constantly affect various markets, including real estate, money, and capital markets, which can enhance or erode whatever we have set aside. If one becomes slack and lazy, it may amount to stoking a fire. You cannot stop a race until you break the tape if you want to win. The race is not yet over. Keep working extremely hard to preserve what you have. The world is filled with many ex-rich men and previously successful people. It's terrible to be a former landlord that now pays rent. It's heartbreaking to be a former car owner who now goes about by public transport. Please do not take your success for granted. Keep nurturing your success by working hard. Remember that hard work and sheer diligence helped you to become successful. You must never abandon that strong quality that got you there. If you change your attitude, your finances will change. If your wealth reduces, you may never live a debt-free life.

4. CONTROL YOUR CHILDREN

Children are young and are often influenced by peer pressure. They don't understand issues about family finances. They just want everything their friends have. My young son returned from school one day and insisted we go on family vacation. Family vacation in December? And he was specific about the location and country. It was not long before we realized some of his classmates from rich parents were planning a vacation. When children see cars of their friends' parents, they want you to buy the same car. When children visit their friends' homes, they silently compare it with theirs. They compare home appliances, phones, tablets, wristwatches, and even quality of meals served in both homes.

You cannot stop children from behaving like other young people. But you must teach your children that income levels differ from family to family. You must teach your children not to copy everything they see their classmates do. You must teach your children that family priorities differ. When my first house was under construction I let all the children know that Daddy was engaging in a key project. Accordingly, many of our consumption items would be drastically cut down. They have now grown up. But they still remember it.

Guide your children and share information freely with them. Let the family work in one accord. Let there be unity of purpose. Don't let outsiders run your home for you. Don't let your children run you into debt. Don't attempt to impress your children and therefore create a debt crisis.

5. EMPLOY FINANCIAL MANAGEMENT TOOLS

Financial management is a social science. It requires skills. Many people have taken credit lines from banks without knowing how to manage them. Finance is an ever-evolving science. You must constantly get updated. You must realize that credit is someone else's money. Using money that is not yours demands extra skill and extra discipline.

For example, some credit cards permit periods of interest-free credit. It is therefore incumbent on you to quickly pay them off before the interest begins to accrue. Understand how the interest on credits are calculated and compounded, and ensure that you read all credit agreements.

When we buy drugs, we carefully read the dosage directions as prescribed by the doctor. If you have never gone to driving school and don't have a driving license, why should you buy a car? Don't just use credit. Understand how it works.

Don't get into new credit without financial skills on how to use the money and repay it. Understanding finance for nonfinance people is critical to escaping debt bondage. It's all right to borrow, but first understand how to use it profitably.

6. SET DEBT BOUNDARIES

Credit extension is a business. I am a banker and an accountant. The biggest asset in the balance sheet of a bank is loans and advances, otherwise referred to as credit. The primary job of most banks is to create credit. Traditional banks make most of their money by lending or extending credit facilities.

Accordingly, banks will offer you all kinds of credit not because they love you but because they want to make money. If you have a good job or you have a successful business, you will notice unsolicited credit offers from various credit-extending institutions. Even stores will offer you credit.

They already have information on you. They know you are credible. They know you have a good job.

The challenge is to determine your boundaries. Do you really need credit? How much credit do you need? If you do need credit, how quickly will you pay it off? How many credit cards do you need? Must your wallet contain five credit cards? Are you aware that you will be tempted to use those cards if you have them? Do you have a defined limit as to the maximum amount of credit you can use at all times? Everything may be good, but not all things are expedient.

Bankers have internal guidance limits also known as unadvised credit limits. It's known only to the bank and its officials. It's the maximum they would allow a customer to overdraw his account beyond the limit advised. It makes sense that you also define a limit on the credit you will use. Never exceed it. If you follow this counsel, you will likely remain debt free on a sustainable basis.

7. UTILIZE PROCEEDS OF DEBT APPROPRIATELY

One way to remain debt free while still using credit is to define clearly the intent and purpose of the loan proceeds at the very beginning of contracting it. Whenever you are taking any form of credit, ask yourself if the main objective of that loan will eventually generate cash from which the credit will be paid. For example, if a person takes a college loan to attend university and obtains a degree, the person would one day get a good job that will pay the loan. If a person takes a loan to purchase a short- or long-term investment, all things being equal, one day the returns from the investment along with the initial capital would be used to pay the loan.

Consider, however, a person who borrows money to buy food for the home. Will that food generate income? Consider a person who borrows money to buy clothing and shoes for personal use. Please explain to yourself the source of cash flow from this consumption expenditure.

Consider a person who uses a credit card to travel all over the world to exotic locations but cannot pay off that loan in six months.

Don't get me wrong. We all need vacations. We all love to travel to places we have not been before. I have personally been to most continents of the world either for business or pleasure. It's fun. I am talking, however, of cutting your coats according to the size of your fabric. Plan your vacations way ahead and save on various cost heads. Booking for an airline ticket one year ahead can save you as much as 50 percent. There are also various kinds of airlines. There are budget airlines that save money. Even within the airlines there are various classes of seats with cost implications. Are you taking advantage of the airline's frequent-flier programs? How about choice of hotels? They come in classes. How about rooms within the chosen hotels? How about local road transportation? Do you consider shared rides and group vacations? When you arrive at your vacation spots, where do you have your meals? Do you know that you can have free breakfast?

Here is the bottom line: be prudent. Don't use credit cards on consumption items except when you know you are only bridging a very temporary gap. It should not be a way of life to use credit for expenses that do not generate cash in the short or long run.

8. ENGAGE IN PERIODIC MONITORING

There is a saying that what does not get measured does not get done. There is great power in looking backward for purposes of corrective actions.

The beginning point is to ensure appropriate planning. That's what I called setting boundaries earlier in this chapter. Set targets and timelines. After you have set the limits, review your actual expenses against the limits. This will indicate to you expense heads where you may have inadvertently overshot the limits. Understand why you exceeded those credit limits. It will be nice to have a sticker on your wall to remind you consistently of the need not to exceed those lines in the future.

Please institute a strong regular monitoring mechanism to ensure you keep a tab on your use of credit lines. I advise you use your paycheck period for purposes of this monitoring. This institutionalized regime of self-appraisal and monitoring has proven to be helpful in keeping oneself in check.

Finally, remember that nobody will do it for you. Only you can do it for yourself. Just make monitoring your finances a part of your life. It may take you about thirty minutes. But it is sure worth the effort and time. You will be glad you did.

9. MAKE SOCIAL INVESTMENTS

Human beings are great social beings. That's how we are configured. We are configured to relate to other humans. They may be our relatives, colleagues at work, or friends. That's why the social media is literally exploding. Humans are configured to keep interacting. Those that ignore this principle get depressed and in some extreme cases could develop mental illnesses.

The way it works is that what you sow is what you get back. Sometimes what you get back will be bigger because the harvest is often bigger than the seed.

It is important that you stay close to your contacts. Attend their functions such as weddings, child dedications, house-warming ceremonies, birthday parties, etc. Assist them as much as you can if they ask for help. Encourage them and give hope when they are down. Our social life demands our investment of time, money, and intellect. If you have lent a helping hand to someone, there is a high probability that someone could lend you a hand when you are down. Somehow what goes around comes around.

One key advice you receive from a true friend could change your life forever. Besides as you relate with many people you will get to know that some things happening in your life may be happening in their lives too. It's possible that they have passed through a similar problem and overcome it. They would readily share their experiences. Critical introductions by valued friends have been the channels through which I have secured most of my jobs including my current job.

Part of the social investment is to engage in community social responsibility. Make impacts in your community. Get involved in community development programs. Begin to volunteer for social work. Help people. Put smiles on the faces of the elderly and destitute. Visit orphanages and prisoners. Make friends with people. Helping the needy has a way of making one content and self-fulfilled as you recognize there are people who are less privileged than you are. This helps to avoid an ostentatious lifestyle. Build a social network. Become socially relevant. Social networks ultimately help in building business networks and could ultimately lead to prosperity and a life that is free of debt.

10. WORK WITH THE PRINCIPLE OF FAITH

When we work hard, sometimes we still fail. Sometimes unexpected misfortunes could arise. In life there are often factors beyond our projections. There is always the unexpected. Some just hit it at the right time. Some work all their lives, but forces beyond their control keep working adversely against them.

Some may call it good luck or ill luck. I believe in God. I believe that one can enjoy favor and blessings from God after you have worked hard with integrity and excellent character. I believe in prayers. That works for me. It has helped me exit debt.

11. BE PATIENT

Credit is often driven by a burning desire to enjoy today rather than wait for the future. If you learn to wait until the future, you are likely to cut down your appetite for credit. If you cut down your appetite for credit, you will likely escape the bondage of debt no matter how often you use credit.

When I had no regular job for about six years, I learned the language of *maintenance*. I learned to maintain my car even though it was falling apart. The temptation would have been to get a new one on credit and complicate my credit headache. I learned to manage old clothes. I learnt to buy fairly used clothes and household accessories instead of buying new ones on credit. I love bicycles. I have been riding bicycles all my life. My favorite bicycle got irreparably broken at the time of my debt crisis. I found a market for secondhand bicycles where I bought one. This unique bicycle is still serving me till now. I even helped some of my friends buy, and made a few bucks, serving as sales agents for similar secondhand bicycles.

Today things have changed radically. I can afford new ones now. But I've learned to be patient. I have learned that the attitude while in the valley should be different from the attitude while one is on the mountaintop. Young people should particularly learn to be patient in life. Those who are passing through debt issues should also learn patience, as debt issues are not resolved overnight. If, however, you are consistent with what you are doing, over time you will discharge your debts and live a sustainable debt-free life.

12. START SMALL BUT THINK BIG

Every big project started small. Every large corporation was once a burning idea in the mind of someone. The person became passionate and began executing the ideas. Gradually results started coming in.

What you see is what you ultimately get. You must begin to dream of a project or job or business that you must do to generate the income that will help you pay your debts.

While dreaming about it as a great project, please start small. Just start. Some have refused to begin. When you begin, please give it all you can give. Anything you give casual attention to will produce suboptimal results. Become extremely passionate about the project. Let the fire of that project burn in your bones. Never make provision for stopping it halfway. If you need help, please humbly seek help. Mobilize all your physical, mental, intellectual, and spiritual resources to make it work. Don't rest until you have a breakthrough. When you have a breakthrough, it will be clear because success cannot be hidden.

But never consider half measures or shortcuts. Take it one step at a time with total commitment, diligence, and perseverance. Some people may despise the days of humble beginnings; I have since learned never to do so. One day you will be so successful in your chosen field of endeavor that you can comfortably pay off your debts and live a sustainable debt-free life.

13. CONSIDER LEGACY ISSUES

I attended a conference recently in Johannesburg, South Africa. The mayor of Johannesburg spoke passionately about the future of the city. Then he delved into his driving force. He kept saying that what keeps motivating him to do more is the future of his grandchildren. I was deeply touched by his statement.

Can I ask you a question? What kind of legacy do you want to leave behind for your children and grandchildren? When you are no longer here, will your children remember you with nostalgia? Will you leave behind assets or liabilities for your children? Will you leave behind reasonable debt-free assets or debts for your children? Will you leave behind a project that will be a source of stream of cash flows for your children and grandchildren, or will you leave behind unpaid bank loans and credit cards? What kind of items can we expect to find in your will?

At the early part of this book I mentioned about my teacher in Long Island City, New York. I mentioned about how his father left him a giant debt-free home, which he sold to buy his first home debt free. He is likely to leave a debt-free home for his own children.

CHAPTER 11

SUSTAINING A DEBT-FREE LIFE

The debtor is literally a slave to the creditor. Living on debt for a lifetime does not confer peace of mind to a reasonable debtor who wants to live debt free. And the problem most of the time is that debtors have few or no ideas on how to escape the debt trap.

No matter your current state of debt exposure, this last chapter will provide you with practical steps you must take now in order to live a life free of debt.

Remember that a temporary use of a credit card that you are sure you will pay off in a reasonably short time does not place you in worrisome debt. The debts you cannot pay in the shortest possible time are the ones that have held you in bondage.

Here are some of the tips that will guide you as you take practical steps to live a debt-free life.

1. CARRY OUT FINANCIAL DIAGNOSIS

Every doctor carries out a complete diagnosis of an ailment before treatment. This may include blood tests and utilization of scanning or other diagnostic equipment. The result of the diagnosis will then determine the line of treatment.

If you are bogged down with financial debts, you will need to do a complete diagnostic review of your finances. You may not be able to solve the problem unless you understand the source. You need to ask what the problem is and find out where the problem originated. You need to do a proper analysis of the debt challenge. You need to ask yourself why you are still in the problem.

The above diagnostic analysis will clearly x-ray the issues around the problem and help you understand what action steps to take in order to resolve the same.

2. TAKE RESPONSIBILITY

There is a tendency to blame others for a debt situation. People blame their ethnic groups, successive governments, the economy, their parents, their spouse, or even their race.

The truth is that none of these are responsible for your debt overhang. You are responsible. You cannot come out of debt if you keep pointing accusing fingers elsewhere. If you blame others, you are likely to look toward that person to solve your problems. Your destiny is in your hands. Even if circumstances beyond your control pushed you into debt, you cannot expect the circumstances to bring you out. You must take responsibility and take positive steps to come out of it.

Consider that you are driving on an icy, slippery road during winter. If you mistakenly skid off the road, it's very easy to blame others for the slippery road. You can blame the road, nature, the weather, or even the car manufacturer. But the fact is that the blame game will not take you out of the ditch. You need to find a way out by yourself. It does not matter how you got into debt. Only you will bring yourself out. You must take responsibility.

3. BELIEVE YOU WILL BE FREE

Taking responsibility is not enough. You must believe that you can come out of debt. Some have thrown their hands up in the air and resigned themselves to fate. Some believe they are born poor and must die poor and remain in debt. Some cannot see a way out and believe it's how they were created to be. They believe nature has poor people and rich people.

What do you believe? Everything is possible to those that believe. It's a battle of the mind. What's your mind telling you? Many people have exited debt. Those that believe will make it. Do not lose the battle of the mind. Your strength is in the mind. If you are defeated on the inside, you will never win outside. If your mind is telling you that there is no need to try and make an effort, you have already lost the battle. Refuse to accept such suggestions. Tweak your mind and set it to believe it can be done. When you believe it, then you are on the way to freedom from debt.

4. BUILD CAPACITY

A man can never operate at a level beyond what he knows. You are what you know. You cannot fly an airplane if you never attended an aviation college to learn how to be a pilot. You can't drive a car safely except you attend a driving school. You cannot go into space except you have gone to NASA to learn about space exploration. You cannot even operate simple devices unless you have thoroughly read and understood the user's manuals. Take time to acquire financial knowledge. Love finance.

Study widely. Get a formal education. If you have not attended university, do not give up. It's not too late. Recently I read of a man who graduated at ninety-three. You can still get into college no matter how old you are today. Look for a community college near you. You may find something interesting. Search for grants, scholarships, or other forms of student aid. Search for online degree programs. Look for universities that could offer summer classes on a weekend or part-time basis. You never know what is available until you search for them.

When did you get your undergraduate degree? How much knowledge have you added to your degree? If you obtained your undergrad degree over twenty years ago, and you have not attended any formal training since then, you are literally stale. You need to update your knowledge. Consider a postgraduate degree on part-time basis. Consider executive education. In one way or the other, enhance your knowledge and enlarge your capacity. You will suddenly discover that you will function better in things you do when you enhance your capacity. You will certainly make better decisions. You will be more productive and certainly more efficient. Knowledge liberates the mind. Get knowledge, and get liberated to function at your best.

5. USE PROFESSIONALS

No matter what you know, you cannot know everything about everything. One piece of evidence that a person is smart is when the person recognizes his/her limitations. Successful people are known to surround themselves with people who are smarter than themselves.

No matter what you know, learn to leverage on the professionals who obviously know more than you. Consult wide. Hire finance professionals and maximize their use. Pay their fees. Retain them for present and future consultations. Interact with them regularly. Never take key finance decisions without consulting the experts. It's worth every fee you pay for it. It will certainly save you heartaches.

6. PREPARE BEFORE ENGAGING IN FINANCE

Every successful outing is a result of long, careful planning. When you attend a wedding party, you may have fun for an hour or two, and it's over. Guess what; that successful party possibly cost weeks of preparation and planning.

Many times we attend weekend games and enjoy sports. The players may play for an hour or even less. What you do not remember is that the players have been practicing since Monday. When we watch live theater programs for about two hours, we don't take note that the actors have spent months rehearsing. Some blockbuster movies we watch may take up to a year to be produced. It's all about preparation.

Preparation reduces unpleasant surprises. Preparation helps you eliminate errors or at least minimize them. Don't dabble into money or financial matters without preparation. Don't rush into real estate or the stock market. Don't embrace credit cards without understanding how and why they are used. If you are already in, step out, pause, and get prepared before you launch in again. No time used in preparation is wasted. Take your time, but be ready.

7. EXIT THE EXPRESSWAY OF EMOTION

Financial issues could bring on negative emotions. Unfortunately, money is neither made nor managed on the platform of emotions. In the same way, we should not be emotional about money handling. The moment you put on your emotional cap in respect to financial matters you put your wealth at risk.

Finance is a serious issue. The accountant who keeps the record of money, the bank manager who keeps money in the vaults of the bank, and the staff in the minting company are all working for money. Attorneys, stockbrokers, and practically everyone in employment work to earn money.

If everyone is laboring to get money, what makes you think you get money through emotions? Wealth creation and preservation requires logical rational reasoning. Therefore, never handle money matters with emotions. It just will never work. Money business is serious business.

8. REFUSE TO FAIL

If it was easy to earn money, everyone would be very wealthy, and nobody would be in debt.

It's not easy, but the problem with the weak is that they give way without a fight. The strong, however, are determined. They never accept no for an answer. They are determined to legally confront all obstacles. They envisage problems on the way, but they never have a plan to surrender.

The English translation of the Latin motto of my high school says, "Either I find the way, or I make one." What that means is that one must be determined to break through no matter the challenges. If you find the way, that's great. If you cannot find the way, then make a new way. Someone told me about a millionaire who was once his employer. This millionaire employer told his employees that if any doors were to be shut, they should make new doors through the walls. As long as your actions are legal and moral, every wall is a potential new door. While one person sees a wall, other smart finance people see a door that will be made through that wall. It takes guts to succeed. You must never let money control you. You must pursue the quest to be financially successful. You must be in charge. Be determined to excel in your profession and business. Be determined and demystify debt. Be determined not to owe. Be determined to pay what you owe. That's the way to live a sustainable debt-free life.

9. START SAVING NOW

I know you wish you had read this book twenty years ago and started saving then. But I have good news for you; today is not too late to start.

Obviously if you had started much earlier you would have accumulated much more with less stress. Imagine if you had been saving five dollars per day for the last forty years. You would have had the sum of $73,000 (excluding interest) safely tucked away in a bank now. If you saved ten dollars per day over the last forty years you would have had $146,000 (without interest).

You can still start saving and accumulate income today. The only thing is that your savings deductions will need to increase. If you need to save $24,000 over ten years, you must save a minimum of $2,400 per year or

$200 per month. If you consider how much you spend on some avoidable nonessentials, you will be amazed that you can achieve that savings target and possibly exceed it. The working strategy is to set the target, start now, and then stay the course.

10. DON'T COVER UP YOUR PROBLEMS

Unfortunately, some people hide their financial problems. They quietly suffer in silence not knowing that a problem revealed is half-solved. Many people hide their debt problems by taking on more debts. If you do not report your medical problems to your doctor, they will definitely degenerate. And after awhile, you may eventually end up in the emergency room. The same applies to debt management.

If you are in a debt crisis or have lost control over your credit card management, you will need help. If you lack discipline to manage credit or you cannot control your desire to keep purchasing unnecessary things, then you will need help. You need counsel, a professional support group, or even peer assistance.

Psychologists may be helpful in curtailing expenses while some may need a mentor or financial consultants. The strategy is to open up and seek help. If you could solve your financial crises by yourself, you would have been out of the problem by now.

11. USE THE TOOLS IMMEDIATELY

You have read so much of the various tools available to avoid the debt trap and to build wealth. You have also read about what you need to do to preserve your wealth or exit the debt trap.

Please do not just be excited about this book. I will obviously be glad if you recommend this book to your friends. But more than this is if you put into practice all that you have learned.

Please find here some examples of a few things you need to do immediately.

- Draw up an implementation plan for all the action items you have identified in this book.
- Set up alarm systems, measurement systems, and monitoring systems. Design what works for you.
- Identify and contact experts that you need to work with for financial success.
- Identify expenses you need to avoid going forward.
- Identify redundant assets you can sell to generate needed cash flow.
- Set your credit card limits.
- Enhance your education even if it means attending university.
- Determine the investments you need to make to grow your wealth.
- Start saving.

Understand that you will not get results unless you act on what you have learned. Please go beyond acquiring knowledge; put that knowledge into practice.

12. ARREST DERAILMENT EARLY

Always watch out for early warning signals. It's easy to arrest problems before they get worse. The moment you start finding it difficult to pay your credit, that is a pointer that all may not be well. It's either that there is a shortfall on your revenue or you have overstretched your spending limits. Whatever is responsible for this circumstance becomes a wakeup call. It's time to investigate. Don't rush to take on additional credit. Taking more credit without resolving the fundamental cause may only aggravate the issue. It may actually be the best time to apply all brakes on major expenses. Thereafter a systemic payment regime can be worked out to pay off the usual credit. Please watch out for early signs and take redemptive actions.

13. BEGIN TO INVEST

The fortunes of a wealthy man cannot be reversed by temporary credit shortfalls. This is because the person has buffers in the form of cash, near cash assets, or even fixed assets that could be disposed of to liquidate maturing credit obligations.

The only way to build such wealth, therefore, is to keep investing. There is no alternative to investments. You must keep investing in hybrid instruments. You must invest in assets that not only protect the original costs but also confer reasonable yields.

Nonetheless, as you invest always rely on expert advice. Keep shifting and shuffling the assets as macroeconomic factors change.

Furthermore, ensure that you protect your wealth. Avoid unnecessary litigations. Take appropriate insurance coverages as are necessary.

14. FORGIVE YOURSELF

In building wealth, we may make mistakes. We can be exposed to unexpected adverse macroeconomic situations. Sometimes some investments become sour due to wrong professional counsel. At other times forecasts or business deals may fail. People could lose their jobs, as once happened to me. Traditional castles could just crumble.

Friends, business associates, and even mentors could disappoint you. Peers could fail you while you may face some unexpected expenses. You may find yourself in a deep financial hole that you never planned for with shrinking revenues and galloping expenses.

The solution lies in you forgiving yourself for any mistakes you may have made and then relaunching yourself. Never write yourself off. No matter the depth of your debt, you can still pay it off. You can still recover the losses you incurred if you keep trying. You must take along with you the lessons you learned and move on. If you write your lessons down as I did, hopefully one day you will write a book like this encouraging others. If I was able to overcome after falling abysmally low in debt, you can overcome too.

15. BE HARD ON YOURSELF

You have always heard people asking you to give yourself a treat. Others say you should spoil yourself and treat yourself like a king. I have a contrary advice: be hard on yourself.

Let me explain. Until you become very wealthy don't get used to excessive fun or relaxation. If you get carried away by early signs of success without holding on tight, you may lose it all, especially with unexpected changes in the environment. Don't celebrate before your time. Continue to work extremely hard and don't slacken while you are in the process of building your wealth. Suspend expensive vacations for as many years as possible. Forget about changing household furniture unnecessarily. Keep fixing broken-down household items. Use small cars or fairly used cars. Avoid expensive clothing or restaurants. While denying yourself of these, work harder at enlarging your income base. Take as many jobs as possible and diversify your income sources.

Following this principle consistently for between seven and ten years will help you build considerable wealth. That will serve as a reasonable buffer when you then decide to start spoiling yourself.

The other unwritten benefit of this lifestyle discipline is that it trains you to exercise self-control. It gives you the capacity to control wealth rather than to let wealth control you. This same principle will enable you to exercise utmost control over the use of your credit cards while keeping your credit under reasonable control.

16. LEARN TO FLY ALONE

Many birds flock together when they fly. However, eagles fly alone. They soar far higher than any other birds. In our environment, credit is everywhere, and unsolicited credit offers are tempting.

Most people are falling for the credit offers, but I advise you to dare to be different. The lure of credit is strong. Please avoid the broad way where the majority are rushing through and discover the narrow way that only very few will find. If all your friends are obtaining several credit cards, you stick with one. If your peers are using their credit cards without restraint, please become the odd one out. If everyone you know is exhausting their savings and migrating to complete credit, please stay strong and determine to be different.

People may call you old-fashioned in a modern world. Remain steadfast. When you finally become debt free and fairly self-sufficient without credit, you will laugh last. As the saying goes, he who laughs last laughs best. No man becomes wealthy by spending borrowed money. Learn to fly alone. Be an eagle!

17. MANAGE THE FAMILY UNIT

The family unit is very powerful. It provides emotional stability and peace of mind to enable you to confront external forces. There is room to support one another within the family unit while facilities and equipment are commonly shared at home. If everyone in the family unit earns a decent income, the family's standard of living should ordinarily be good.

On the other hand, when there are uncoordinated expenses and lifestyles in the home, the family unit may be negatively affected. Emotional instability in the home could also affect general productivity and possibly create debts. It could even get far worse in cases of divorce. Cost of litigations could be unbearable. Child support costs could negatively affect one's credit and lifestyle.

With these in mind, make every effort to keep the family unit intact. It provides financial mutual support. It serves as a restraining factor for the spendthrifts. The family unit provides emotional support that would ginger you to succeed. It helped me a lot in my darkest moments. It could also help you.

18. KEEP AT IT

Exiting debt is a process. It's a journey. It's not an event. It requires patience. Please understand that there is no magic wand that takes a debt burden away. Careful and consistent application of the principles enunciated in this book will definitely assist. Of course, a lot depends on you. When you start the process you need to see it through until you achieve the desired results. As you achieve results, continue to do the right things to remain debt free on a sustainable basis.

The most important thing is to start the journey. In order to start the journey, you can start "sealing your leaking pockets" by cutting down your expenses. Once you start boosting your incomes, then you keep paying the debts. Just keep at it. Even when you get a higher-paying job, you must overcome the temptation of raising your lifestyle.

CONCLUSION

Please do everything you can to avoid driving on the highway of debt. If you are already entrapped in debt, take positive steps to get out. Clearly you can now see that there are many exit points out of recalcitrant debt. Seek financial knowledge, work with financial consultants, and obtain quality undergraduate and postgraduate education. Furthermore, there is the need to develop the right attitude as it concerns finance and debt.

That's not enough to exit debt. You also need to achieve financial security by building and preserving personal wealth. Furthermore, you must take practical steps on a consistent basis that will enable you live a debt-free life on a sustainable basis.

One final word: you are the CEO of your financial life. Make good decisions and plan your future. Make tough and timely decisions. Be deliberate and consistent in your decisions. If you do all the above, I am confident that you will not only exit debt, you will build sufficient personal wealth that would enable you to achieve financial freedom.

I recommend you to finish well and finish strong. The end of anything is more important than its beginning. If you want to leave a great legacy for your children, then you must work toward it. Map out the plan. Keep working toward it. Set yearly targets for yourself. Refuse to be discouraged.

When you fall, rise up and keep trying. Employ all resources at your disposal. Seek the ones you do not have but which you will need. Be humble. Remain determined. Go for the best. One day you will look back and say that you have fought a good fight and that you have finished your course well. I congratulate you in advance.

Notwithstanding the credit craze, we can always live a good life without being enslaved in debt. Develop the right attitude and obtain a good education. Run your home with financial intelligence. Apply the principles of the CEOs of corporations. If they work for corporations, they will work for you.

Learn to save. It may not be popular today because of the craze for credit. It is, however, an age-old principle for building reserves and wealth. Begin to build wealth now. Finally, be prudent. Never let your expenses outweigh your income.

I am confident that one day the world will read your own book of testimonies and that you will be able to build and sustain wealth. If you apply the principles in this book, I am confident you will run your financial life like successful corporations do.

You have already learned principles that could entrap people in debt; please avoid them. You now know how to exit debt if you are already entrapped. You have learned how to cope in a world of credit. Live it.

Initiate and sustain a culture of living out of debt bondage.

The time to act is now.

Printed in the United States
By Bookmasters